EXIT 8

How Battered Women
STAY OUT

16 Domestic Violence Survivors
Reveal Their Long-Term Struggles
AND Solutions for a
NEW Life **FREE of** Abuse

Mary Walker Owens M.A.

Family Sociology/Criminology
Domestic Violence Worker/Survivor

<u>How Battered Women Stay Out</u>

GREAT SKY PUBLISHING

ISBN: 1497502993
ISBN-13: 978-1497502994

DEDICATION

TO IYANLA VANZANT

Beloved Sister Survivor,

When I saw you on television that day, I saw in you, both me - and the me I wanted so much to be ...

When I read your books, I prayed for peace of mind and especially for the forgiveness that you said you experienced in the chapel - that day ... as you stood over your abuser's lifeless body.

When I finally returned to college, fighting constant panic attacks, physical injuries and PTSD, I played your CD "In the Meantime" every single day while driving to campus - my hands sweating on the steering wheel. Your calming voice, your affirming words - constantly with me ...

You kept me safe ... you got me there ...

You comforted me on every single mile of my journey.

And when I finally began listening to and recording the stories of other abuse survivors for this book, I placed your powerful words on my desktop screen.

I began my work - every single time reading the following words ... YOUR words ... as you continued to cheer me on ... and like a loving mother to encourage me ...

> *If you do it all for God - in Excellence and in Truth,*
> *He will reward you. Tell Your Story. It will heal*
> *you - and someone else ...*   Iyanla Vanzant

THANK YOU SO MUCH

How Battered Women Stay Out

CONTENTS

ACKNOWLEDGEMENTS

INTRODUCTION   1

"Wrap It Up Rayette" by Ami Cannon, Survivor   4

PART I LONG TERM SURVIVORS   5
        "Someday" by Aylin Belle Amie, Survivor   6

     2 MY JOURNEY BEGINS   7

        What Was Missing?   13

     3 MEET THE SURVIVORS   20
        Survivor Biographies
        The Interview Sessions

PART II TALKING TO LONG TERM SURVIVORS   27
        "From Now On" by Lee Michael   28

     4. SURVIVORS TALK ABOUT STAYING OUT   29
        BETWEEN TWO WORLDS
        GOAL ORIENTED BEHAVIOR   30
            Positive Self Evaluation
            Learning Effective Problem Solving
            Avoiding Potential Abusers
            Having a Higher Quality of Life:

     5. SOCIAL SUPPORT AND CONNECTION   45
        BASIC NEEDS
        Safety, Shelter, Children, Medical/Mental

ACKNOWLEDGMENTS

The real credit for the completion of this book belongs to the sixteen long-term domestic abuse survivors who shared their stories with me. They generously gave me their time, opened their hearts, and bared their souls, so that this book could become a reality. The honesty with which they related their struggles, frustrations and their pain, along with their learned wisdom and achievements, have provided us with a meaningful contribution to domestic violence research.

My gratitude is also extended to the staff of Haven House in Pasadena, Forrest Atkins, of the Department of Rehabilitation, and most recently Ellen, and the staff of Safe Nest in Las Vegas Nevada. Credit is also due to Dr. Richard Merrill, Dr. Amy Jaffey, and Dr. Heino Lange, three devoted medical professionals, whose skilled counseling, love and patience, comprised an essential part of my own healing and recovery from domestic abuse.

My appreciation also goes to Dr. Helen Meloy, Dr. Jane Prather, Dr. Vickie Jensen and Dr. Marta Gaffney, and to my fellow writers in the OLLI Creative Writing Group at UNLV. Their enthusiasm, encouragement, and guidance have been pivotal and continued sources of inspiration for me. Thank you to Cathy Lowe, and to my talented OLLI friends, for their assistance in proofreading: Ruth Elliot, Martha Carrel, Lynne Boone and Louise Wrice. My gratitude is expressed also, to musician and author Larry "Wild" Wrice and to Charles Boone, who both helped me get Great Sky Publishing off to a fantastic start.

Thank you, to the Maryvale Girls, and my deep gratitude is extended to Ami Cannon, talented writer, composer, singer, and actress for her proofreading assistance and support. Appreciation also goes out to Aileen Rochester, another sister survivor, skilled health professional, writer, singer, and poet. To these women, to the Haven House Outreach sisterhood and to the members of Dr. Jaffey's Women's Group - thank you all so much for cheering me on, until I finally reached the finish line

I want to also express sincere thanks and mountains of love to my three children, who stood with me, all the way down the road, through my escape from violence and recovery. Thank you also, to my eight grandchildren and first great grandchild, who have all been sources of unending love and constant inspiration. The love we all share together - the sheltering warmth of having been blessed with the beautiful, non-violent, close family despite the challenges of single motherhood, has been the wind beneath my wings.

Thank you is long overdue also to Kevin, a man of peace and non-violence, who always cared about my goals, assisted me in accomplishing them, and remained a true friend. Deep appreciation to Sherman, Eric, and to my son Thomas, all peaceful warriors, and artists - men who still strive everyday to annihilate the fires of hatred, with the perpetual, glowing spirit of creativity and love. Love and gratitude always to Terence, my fellow author, soul mate, poet and muse,

To all of these very special people, and especially to my cousin Thom, who gave me my first typewriter in 1964, and who never stopped believing in me - I dedicate this book

INTRODUCTION

Leaving an abusive relationship, and gaining the necessary resources for survival, can present a real challenge for women. This is especially true, if domestic violence shelter or services are not available, or are not utilized. Domestic violence researchers, and other concerned communities, have shed light on the problems survivors often face *after* they leave. In this book, I offer to readers, what I have learned from many hours of interviews and caring communication with long term survivors of domestic violence (see Chapter 2 for a definition of "long term survivor"). These women have generously offered first-hand, intimate accounts of their experiences of abuse, escape, rescue, and recovery, along with their wisdom and personal advice. They have also provided suggestions for improvement in the larger social systems that they have navigated, and attempted to obtain assistance from for several years. These sixteen long term survivors, themselves, have offered their own, valuable, expertise and advice for victims, survivors, and members of the larger society who have been and will be affected by this very serious issue.

My study of these courageous women also includes an in-depth compilation, and summary of prior domestic violence research by many experts in this field. Among these, are college professors, counselors, psychologists, feminists, sociologists and others. The insights gained from their findings will offer readers a large accumulation of useful information that is valuable to victims and survivors of domestic abuse, as well as to their caring friends, and family members. Students, researchers, and those simply interested in learning more about this very important topic, will also find my book helpful. Chapter 10 offers readers a broad overview of the prevalent and more prominent psychological and therapeutic approaches. Social welfare and feminist solutions for solving the problem of domestic violence are also presented in this Chapter. Chapter 11 provides an in depth sociological analysis of the insights gained from talking to survivors through the application of Symbolic Interaction and Social Process theories.

During my initial research, and as my interviews with survivors, and coding of data progressed, my own experience as a domestic violence survivor merited contemplation. Being a survivor of spousal abuse, myself, it was easy for me to empathize with the experiences, and emotions that were described, and expressed to me by those with whom I spoke. In some cases, I could not help but be moved, and sometimes even angered, when hearing about the acts of physical, verbal, mental, and sexual abuse these survivors had endured, in some cases, for most of their lives. Although feminist research methodology provides formal justification for allowing one's own perspective and experience into an interview and analysis, I still felt the need to guard against influencing the women I talked to with my own bias. As one prominent domestic violence expert has remarked, researchers always tend to find what they are looking for (Bowker 1993). I am pleased to state that my own fear of excessive personal, or undue bias, began to evaporate, as the interviews progressed, when many unexpected findings began to unfold before me.

These victims and survivors of domestic violence definitely had strong opinions, and perspectives that were uniquely their own. Some of their viewpoints even surprised me. As a somewhat politicized survivor, who is also a sociologist, I had expected to hear, in my interviews with survivors, great frustration and anger directed at the social support agencies that are supposed to assist abused women and children. Instead, I learned about the other deep, ongoing concerns many of these long term survivors shared. As a result, I was forced to alter my own perspective about the long-term experience of formerly abused women, along with the particular ways in which they seek, and perceive of support.

It is my aspiration that, in this book, I have honored the great sociological traditions of feminist methodology and grounded theory analysis. Through these approaches, I have attempted to provide in-depth descriptions, using the words of the women, themselves, of the experience of being victims, and then   long term survivors - and of the value and importance of social support in their lives.

I offer this study – my dedicated in-depth research, and the heartbreaking, yet inspiring interviews that follow, to women who are now being abused, in the hope that they, too, will get out, and stay out - that they, too - will become Survivors.

I offer my work to those women who have finally taken the courageous step to leave. Keep the faith – you'll make it!

I offer this work to victims' family members, experts in the field, and even to batterers, who are themselves, often victims of prior childhood abuse.

I offer this book to the universe, along with my prayers, in a spirit of love, peace, non-violence, empathy, healing, and greater understanding.

Wrap It Up Rayette

Wrap it up, Rayette. Leave him tonight
You got the guts and you got the fight
Wrap it up, Rayette. Head for the door
and he ain't gonna hurt you anymore

What's the picture playing on your mind?
Mama in the bedroom cryin' one more time.
"It's nobody's business" they said back then,
"Just grit your lip, now don't talk back,
Shh! Count to ten."

Daddy was so lovely (right?) when he wasn't Mr. Hyde,
born of wounds and memories and fears inside.
I'm sorry for Daddy but it was no excuse
to go half-cocked and brain dead, locked,
and turn the fury loose.

Remember your beauty, remember who you are –
a lover, a giver, God's shining star.
You deserve to be in all your crown and glory.
It's time now, woman, for a brand new story.

©Music and Lyrics by
Ami Cannon, Survivor

PART ONE

LONG TERM SURVIVORS

SOMEDAY

Someday soon, if only in my nearly captive mind
I can run to a place where feel safe
From the bondage of the harmful one
I'll be able to escape the torment and
Stop fading into invisible nothingness

Someday soon if only in distracted dreams,
I'll fly away to a place so distant,
Speak a language unknown,
Dress and look differently,
And feel like a native of another land.

Someday soon, if only in the promises of my heart,
I will be born again slowly;
Growing separate from my downtrodden being
How I will flourish in the shelter of the new me
Which will let me live without fear.

Someday soon, in dress rehearsals from a trapped life,
Will come the clarity of what could be gained
From a seeking of worthiness and love
Given by a safe, respectful world
When reflected on me, gives me back life itself.

Someday soon,
I will be free,
Someday…
So soon…

© Aylin Belle Amie, 2113
Survivor, *from her book*
"Nature Lights My Soul"

6

CHAPTER ONE

MY JOURNEY BEGINS

Over ten years ago, I embarked upon a journey of discovery. I wanted to find out how battered women who leave their abusers go on to successfully rebuild their lives. I wanted to understand how some women avoid future victimization after leaving, and why others repeat the same self-destructive patterns again and again. My motivation was up close and personal. I was one of those abused women who finally summoned the courage to escape from my violent partner and run for my life. Did I possess special "survivor" qualities that had enabled me to avoid future abuse: to "get out and stay out"? Or, was I just plain lucky? In the 1970's when I fled my batterer, the topic of spousal abuse or wife-beating was seldom talked about. Women still hid their bruises and emotional scars, coping secretly with humiliation and shame. Some of our mothers and grandmothers had hidden that same embarrassment for many years before us. Thankfully, battered women today have finally found a voice, through the efforts of feminist advocates and other caring communities. Many women, like me, have broken the chains of victimization that bound us. We now proudly refer to ourselves as "survivors"– a title earned through fierce determination and courage.

The average abused woman tries to leave her abuser at least five to seven times – eventually going back to him - until she finally ends the cycle of abuse in her life (Prime zone Media Network, 2005). That is why this book is called "Exit Eight: How Battered Women STAY OUT." It is not about just "getting away" - it is about "staying away". Sixteen survivors who have met this challenge and succeeded will reveal their challenges, strategies, and solutions, sharing with readers what they experienced and how they rebuilt their damaged lives after leaving – never to be abused again. I bravely escaped my abuser one very frightening night, after five years of his abuse and many, many failed attempts to leave. My actual departure that evening had been very carefully planned. I left him with only the clothes on my back, a few belongings, and my precious children. Unfortunately, my post-exit life was not so accurately predicted and organized. The day following my departure, I woke up after two hours of troubled sleep, with an unsettling realization. In two more weeks, I would have no safe place to stay with my children. Many sleepless nights followed; extreme fear and anxiety caused my mental and physical health to quickly deteriorate. Eventually, after many hysterical phone calls, the Red Cross referred me to a battered women's' shelter in Southern California. During my 30 day stay there, I was assisted in many ways by a network of caring domestic violence professionals to finally begin the process of restoring my well-being and rebuilding my life. I would soon change my name and remain hidden from my abuser for many years. After his repeated threats to kill me, I was terrified that he would find us and hurt me - and our children.

I was so frightened of him that when I rented an apartment a few months later, I slept on the floor, with my body pressed up against the front door blocking it from entry for nearly a year. I would also find out from former neighbors, that my batterer's anger, after my departure, had become even more explosive. To make matters worse, his violence had escalated and become greatly exacerbated due to his alcoholism and worsening paranoid illness. My brief shelter stay, along with intermittent counseling was the only sources of help available to me at that time, and during the years that followed. My own difficulty in obtaining needed resources was not unique. It mirrored the experience of many other victim/ survivors of domestic abuse during the last century who, like me were also unable to receive adequate assistance. Sadly, society's failure to adequately address and punish domestic violence crimes still adversely affected many victims when I began researching data for this book. As the 20TH century ended, severe violence or wife beating[1] was still being suffered by over 1.8 million women each year (Gelles, 1997); another later report revealed that Intimate Partner Violence (IPV) had become a public health epidemic, affecting nearly 32 million Americans each year (Tjaden & Thoennes, 2000a).

During the 1990s, more attention to the topic of domestic violence evolved, as the famed O.J. Simpson Case illuminated on household television sets the raw, ugly, severity of the problem of wife beating. Millions of shocked viewers in outrage began to press for new legislation to provide more assistance for abused women. As a result, many police officers and judges have more tools with which to protect and help victims and their families and to aggressively prosecute batterers. Today's media now frequently features human interest stories about domestic abuse. Optimism is growing that the larger society is actually beginning to care about domestic violence. Yet, the fact still remains that, when a victim finally exits an abusive relationship, he, or she is not only impacted by the dangers presented by the batterer himself or herself. Many challenges remain during the process of attempting to obtain adequate assistance and social support. Many victims have survived their partner's abuse, only to confront a new mountain of problems and what could be termed, in some cases, even institutional abuse, or neglect.

Some of these problems can persist for years. My own long-term experience, after leaving my batterer, convinced me this was true. Among various "post exit" obstacles in my own life were bouts with poverty, homelessness, lack of transportation, battered women's syndrome, anxiety disorders, failed relationships, and persistent terrifying panic attacks. During my later employment as a hot-line counselor at a battered women's shelter, I discovered that these and other difficulties were very common among most survivors "post-exit". What was even more problematic for me as a survivor, was the fact that even years later, I would continue to confront these, along with new challenges with my children. Most of these difficulties were directly related to my former domestic abuse. I was raising our son, once named lovingly after his father: a wonderful little boy, and later a young man, without a father as a role model. And causing me even more distress, were constant conflicts, and arguments almost weekly, which went on for years with our beautiful daughter. She deeply resented me for the pain she endured from not being able to see her biological father. She insisted to me, repeatedly, that she be allowed to find him - even though I told her again and again, that he would potentially be very dangerous to all of us. I began to wonder as I struggled and survived over the years, if there were other women who were also experiencing persistent problems like mine (especially those I was enduring with my daughter) even years after fleeing their own abusers.

I began to look for answers to my questions from other women, like myself, who had managed to not only get out of their relationships, but to STAY OUT. I began searching for a sort of "survivor sisterhood", whom I would later define as "long term survivors". I started paying close attention to news stories and interviews that featured survivors of domestic abuse, now also called "intimate partner violence" (IPV) in newspapers and on television. I also read several books on the subject and talked to other victims and survivors whenever I could. I began attending police and medical information meetings and joined women's' groups, where I could ask more questions whenever the subject arose. I also attended therapy regularly, where I was able to gain additional in-depth understanding about my own experiences as both a victim of abuses and as a "long term survivor".

Later, when I returned to college, I perused nearly every academic journal article that had been written about domestic violence. The more I read and asked questions, the more additional questions about the topic began to emerge in my mind. What I finally realized was that no one, at that time, had really provided a complete picture of how women who fled abusive men actually learned to navigate the new social worlds and systems they found themselves newly reliant upon. We also did not really have a complete "close-up" picture of the subjective world of the formerly battered woman and of her metamorphosis into a "survivor". What went on in her mind, as she moved toward empowerment and independence? What were her concerns? And how she avoid future abuse, over the long term - and "stay away"? How did she actually gain effective support? What actually worked for her? What strengthened her and, conversely, what threatened her well being? What did she think jeopardized her potential for successful recovery and empowerment after she left?

As far as I could see, after months of dedicated research, those questions and other related issues had not really been adequately addressed. I decided that I needed to start talking to survivors myself in order to learn the answers, but I still was not completely certain of how I should proceed. How would I find women who were willing to talk about their experiences as former victims and, more importantly, as survivors? Would survivors be afraid to disclose their personal and often painful experiences? Would they be interested in sharing their strategies and solutions? Or would these women be focused primarily on putting their abuse behind them and resent my proposed intrusion into their new lives? I was certain that the information I could glean from them would be helpful and to many victims, survivors, and families who have suffered from abuse. Still, I hesitated to proceed.   Then finally, one windy afternoon in San Francisco what I later came to consider my "mission" became very clear. A life-changing incident occurred - dictating to me that I *must* talk to other survivors and write this book.

Describing this life changing event still leaves me nearly breathless. It was totally unexpected: a shocking surprise encounter with my batterer - the man I had hidden from at that point in time, for over 26 years. After confronting him, I discovered that he *had* actually spent those years after I left, waiting, and wanting to kill me. In fact, he still wanted - and intended to kill me on that day. My meeting with him came, seemingly, out of nowhere. I was attending a sociology convention and had left the hotel for a lunch break. Life was good and it was a beautiful day. I was walking down Powell Street toward Market Street and what can only be called a serendipitous event happened. Or was it a miracle? After running away and hiding from him for so many years – I, unknowingly, walked straight to my batterer!

The man I had once loved so much, the father of my children, the person who had beaten me and vowed to kill me, was now a nearly blind homeless man pushing a shopping cart. He looked at me, holding his hand out, as if hoping for some spare change. As he limped to approach me, I could see sores all over his arms and face. Time was suddenly frozen. Everything went into slow motion, as I held my own hand out to give him the coins he had already noticed in my hand. Could this really be him? It couldn't be! I timidly asked his name. Yes, it was really him! Oh no! Now, will he recognize me? His eyes were so cloudy - almost as if they were covered with gauze. Maybe he wouldn't. Would he

11

hurt me? Would he kill me, as he always promised he would? This terrifying encounter did not culminate until nearly 24 hours later. And soon after that life changing day, I would begin to ask myself over and over again, why that horrifying encounter would happen to me on that fateful day.

Why would I suddenly "accidentally" run into the man who I had run and hid from for over 26 years? How could this happen in a place that was 800 miles away from the city where we had lived together when I fled from him? Why was he standing right there, on that particular street, on that particular day? And why was I meant to confront him on the very same day that I was celebrating my own very hard earned mid-life success in graduate school? Could our confrontation *really* have been purely coincidental? I did not think so, as our meeting would not stop replaying in my mind. I remembered hearing one of my heroines, Oprah Winfrey say many times that there are actually no such things as accidents or coincidences in life. Both she and Iyanla Vanzant, who I call my "sister survivor" had been my heroines for many years. "Yes, I thought to myself. Yes, Oprah. Yes, Iyanla - you are both right … yes … seemingly 'accidental' moments in time are not coincidental. They do sometimes carry a very special meaning.

Yes, but if your words of wisdom are true, then what did this totally unexpected, shocking encounter with my prior abuser so many years later really mean? Deep down in my soul, I knew it was a gift of some kind – but why was it given to me *at this moment in time?* I continued to ask myself the same question, repeatedly, until I finally became completely certain of what the answer was. I knew for certain why this remarkable meeting occurred: it happened to let me know that I was meant to tell the untold stories of long term survivors – about LIFE after a woman finally says "beat me now more" - even after 2, 3, 4 or 5 - or even 20 failed attempts to leave - not only does she get out, but she finally STAYS OUT and builds an entirely new life.

So, on that very frightening, but serendipitous, maybe *miraculous* day, this book – "EXIT EIGHT" - was born.

CHAPTER TWO

WHAT WAS MISSING?

B efore I began my interviews with actual survivors, I would first explore in depth, what prior research by experts had already uncovered about life after leaving an abuser. I perused all of the information I could find about the practical and emotional challenges that commonly affect victims before, and especially *after* they leave their batterers. I spent months reading and organizing over one hundred domestic violence books and articles spread across multiple perspectives. Among these were the feminist, sociological, social welfare, criminology, and psychiatric communities. The latter approach is predominant in clinical, and popular literature, having informed many of the counseling and therapeutic methods used today for short and long-term counseling of victims and survivors. Many studies focused on the subjective processes leading to the victim's final "exit" - in other words her eventual decision to leave and begin life on her own. Others highlight the victim's projected or actual difficulties, such as fear of being found by the abuser, homelessness, safety concerns, social isolation, child custody issues, financial hardships, and obtaining affordable housing.

Research also indicated to me that, when victims did finally leave, they were often faced with additional problems getting the appropriate assistance they needed. Lack of sufficient help and protection was often due to shortcomings of law enforcement, social, and legal service providers (Berk 1993; Bowker 1993; Raphael 2000). Obtaining needed services from medical and mental health providers was also very hard for survivors. They also experienced problems in the workplace, and sometimes difficulties interacting with significant others (Murphy 1997; Walker 1994). These issues, along with my other related findings are discussed further throughout the following chapters of this book. Yet, as I proceeded further, delving deeply into all of the available literature I could find, I still remained unable to locate much information

13

about life after leaving – about *what actually happened* to survivors of domestic violence *after they* left their abusers *and over the long term.*

I surmised there might be several reasons for this lack of long term, or "follow-up" information. Domestic abuse was a relatively new social issue at the time: the first domestic violence shelter was not established until 1968 - and even then, the topic was not discussed much. During the seventies, as the shelter movement began to grow in the United States, some studies of victims were conducted at these safe havens. In fact, I actually was personally interviewed, for one such study, as a resident in one such domestic violence shelter in 1976, shortly after I escaped my abuser. Another reason for the lack of information about survivors after they left was, as I had predicted, that these women could be very difficult to find. After exiting abusive relationships, they often remain hidden, or are in a hurry to just go on and begin their new lives. Some women begin life anew and never look back; some women return home to their mate - only to endure further abuse. Other women are in jails or prison for finally performing acts of criminal violence themselves, in self defense or in retribution upon their mates. Some victims are lost among the homeless population, or in some cases, forced to escape to other countries.

According to some experts, effective methodologies for studying the survivor population also have typically been too complex and too costly to conduct within academic communities (Bard 1994, Bowker 1993). I was encouraged, however, to find that several domestic violence advocates and researchers had agreed that a higher priority be placed on better understanding how formerly battered women had ended victimization, and reconstructed their lives (Bowker 1993; Ellis 1992; Browne 1997). During my preliminary research, I did locate a very limited number of prior studies that offered a more expanded view of the victim/survivor's experience over the long term (Bowker 1993; Campbell, Miller and Cardwell 1994; NiCarthy 1987; Statman 1990; Van Zant 1998). These "survivor accounts", which are very rare in domestic violence literature, were usually presented as "case" or "qualitative" studies.

One pioneer study was Gina NiCarthy's (1987) study of thirteen women who "got away" from their abusers and became active agents in changing their own lives. They endured many difficulties after they left. Ex-husbands continued to pursue some of them, while other survivors experienced bouts of loneliness, and financial hardship. Another interesting study was Lee Ann Hoff's (1990) in depth look at *Battered Women as Survivors*. Hoff provided a close-up look at nine survivors of domestic violence, and the members of their formal and informal support networks. Noted expert Kathleen Ferraro (1983) also provided a more expanded look at the post-shelter experiences of a larger group of 120 women. She concluded that surviving spousal abuse and gaining autonomy could be a real struggle for victims.

> "If success is defined in terms of life satisfaction [positive relationships with others, self confidence and optimism about the future], only 30 of the 120 women we met during the study period could be said to have successfully dealt with their battering. An additional 30 women did not return to their marriages, to anyone's knowledge, but continued to face severe problems either financially interpersonally or emotionally. The other 60 shelter residents [who accounted for 50 percent of the sample] returned to their marriages. "(Ferraro 1985)

Another interesting study was *Getting Out: Life Stories of Women Who Left Abusive Men* (1999) by Anne Goetting. Using a life history approach and accounts from women who left, she skillfully created an intimate feminist analysis of survivors' long-term experience before, during, and after their relationships with abusers. Goetting's work also illuminated the harsh reality that, even financially advantaged and young women were not exempt from becoming victims of abuse. "Getting out" could involve more than one exit, and did not happen without great personal guilt, hardship and expense. Goetting stated:

> "professionals lose patience with women's repeated requests for services and so blame them for their victimi-

zation … the more support, rather than blame she encounters along the way the more intact she will be when she reaches that finish line" (Goetting 1999:15)".

Survivor Chronicles

I would be remiss if I failed to mention the overwhelming amount of domestic violence or IPV (Intimate Partner Violence) information made available to the public on popular media outlets in what I will call "Survivor Chronicles". These are very dramatic sometimes heroic accounts of how brutalized victims finally "make it out" or "get away" from their abusers. The media blitz surrounding the Simpson trial gave birth to many "television survivors" who provided an exciting mix of "horror" and public information for talk show viewers. Transformed from victims to survivors, they frequently offered their own biographies and self-help books to readers. Some guests were provided by their hosts with generous "after-care" therapy and other services. Because of their appearances and raw truth-telling, popular media managed to tear away the veil of secrecy that had been placed over domestic violence crimes in the past. However, despite the media spotlight, after each television program ended viewers still were not given the opportunity to view the actual, real social and subjective world domestic violence survivors inhabit and navigate day after day for a long time.

Survivor Chronicles also became plentiful in popular books, newspapers, magazines, crime show programs and more recently, in made-for-television films. Some of these thrilling stories begin or end in murder. Others scripts have heroic "Rocky" style endings where the frightened former victim becomes strong, independent and sometimes even warrior-like (i.e."Enough" starring Jennifer Lopez). Some films have fairytale endings, wherein the survivor meets a non-abusive romantic interest who falls in love with and rescues her (i.e. "Safe Haven" which starred "Dancing with the Stars" favorite Juliette Hough). Although I really enjoyed watching these films immensely, sometimes even crying, as I cheered my heroine on, I still couldn't help but notice, as a former victim/survivor myself that a large gap existed between most media portrayals and the real lives of actual domestic violence survivors.

Most women are neither helpless victims nor heroic martial artist conquerors. Most victims do not look like actresses and do not get rescued by Prince Charming. Most scripts do not tell the stories of the practical obstacles and fears the survivor faces, day after day, as she struggles toward empowerment and independence.

So What Was Still Missing?

I was now very optimistic that the everyday women I would interview for my book could contribute greatly to what was previously known about survivors by adding their own long term, real world insights and wisdom. The list of questions I had begun to ask before encountering my abuser was growing and I was now eager to seek out what I started to refer to as long term survivors, like myself - experts in their own right. I was certain they would provide many answers. I wanted to ask them about all of their experiences post-exit, to explore each woman's unique personal account of life after they left and learn about their long-term needs. I wanted to know so many things. Were their needs ever met, and if so, how? What were their experiences like with dating, with meeting new men? What were their day by day challenges with raising often fatherless children? Were their families helpful? How did they honestly evaluate the institutions that served them, initially, as victims, and later, as survivors, over the long-term?

I was also very curious to ask each woman when and how she actually determined that she was a *"survivor"*. At what point did this transformation from a *"victim mentality"* happen? Or did she ever gain that:*"survivor"* certainty and confidence? What were her evolving perceptions of herself during this process? How does she *stay a "survivor"*? Why does she think this empowering transformation happen for some women, and not for others? So, now finally, I would begin the task of finding women who had actually "gotten away" and "stayed away" so that I could answer these and many other questions. How would I find these survivors and get them to talk to me? The elusive nature of this particular group, along with its' relative exclusion from investigation, presented a real challenge.

But, very journey must begin with a first step.

17

Finding "Long Term Survivors"

The term "long term survivor," would require a preliminary working definition, before I could begin recruiting women who would share their experiences. So, my first step, before I began my interviews, was to define, exactly, what a "long terms survivor" actually was. After careful research and forethought, I would define "long term survivor" as "*a woman who has exited a relationship involving emotional and physical abuse from a spouse or domestic partner, and has not returned to cohabitation with this person, for a period of at least 3 years*". I determined that establishing a *minimum "time gone", after the "exit", of 3 years* would indicate that the abuse survivor had terminated the relationship, permanently, or at least, it would imply a sincere effort to avoid going back to the abuser. (A more in-depth explanation of the process I used to define exactly what a long term survivor was is provided in Appendix A at the end of this book). _

I also wanted to formulate more specific working definitions for the terms "exit", "mate", and "abuse". "Exit", I initially defined as: *leaving the abusive household, or as forcing the abuser to leave.* As the interviews progressed, however, it became apparent to me that some survivors had experienced multiple relationships that included physical and emotional abuse. Because of this, I needed to establish a common survivor "exit" point. I designated this as *the first time the survivor left any abusive "mate".* A "*mate*", for the purposes of my interviews, would be *the first abusive husband or domestic partner with whom the survivor had lived with, independently, after leaving their home.* "Physical *abuse*" was loosely defined as *the intentional, willful, infliction of physical injury on another, by hitting, beating, shoving, and/or pushing.* "Emotional abuse" was defined as *the infliction of emotional hurt by using degrading remarks, insults, dominating behavior, threats, silence, and/or isolation*

After years and years of forethought and research, asking myself more and more questions, it was now, finally time for me to learn answers by speaking to long term survivors firsthand. As stated earlier, a more extensive explanation of the methods I used to find survivors who were willing to talk to me is available for readers who may want additional information in the Appendices at the end of this book. I also have provided readers with an overview of the wealth of available literature about victim/survivors of domestic abuse from both the professional, clinical, and academic communities in Part 3 of this book. This information is drawn from over one hundred behavioral science, academic and popular media references which are all cited and listed at the end of the book.

However, this book is primarily about listening, firsthand, to sixteen survivors of domestic abuse, themselves - and about being able to benefit and gain understanding from the learned wisdom and practical advice they were able to share with us. From these often heartbreaking, informative, and inspiring interviews, we can comprehend, more precisely, what survivors actually experience and overcome, as they begin to reconstruct their lives.

So, now, I am very enthusiastic and proud to introduce you to some very courageous women – the sixteen long term survivors of domestic abuse that I spent many months getting to know - and to deeply respect.

\

CHAPTER THREE

MEET THE SURVIVORS

BETTY was a 33 year old, African-American, female, survivor, who had left her abusive mate 13 thirteen years earlier. At the time of our interview, she had been married to her new husband for 12 years. She described herself as very happy. She said that her new relationship is not abusive, although she and her partner have sometimes come close to "losing control of themselves", during a heated argument. Betty had also experienced childhood abuse. She had a high school education, and some college. She had been working at a battered women's shelter, and was a foster parent, as well as an adoptive mother. She was very proud of her blended family of eight children; she considered being a mother a full-time job.

CASSANDRA was a 32 year old, African-American, female, survivor. She was a college student, and mother of one child, who had left her abusive mate three years before our interviews. She had not been abused or beaten by a man, again, after she left. She would soon receive her Master's Degree, and planned to go on for her Ph.D. At the time of our interview, Cassandra had also enjoyed gainful employment for more than 14 years. She described her childhood as normal, and reported no incidents of childhood abuse or victimization. She was living with her parents, in their household, which also included one of her siblings, and her two year-old son.

CATHY was a 39 year old, Caucasian female, survivor who had left her abusive mate 8 years before I interviewed her. She had been in two serious relationships with men, since then. She described these men as not abusive, although both of them had, each, actually hit Cathy, once, during an argument. Interestingly, she described these incidents as not abusive. Instead, she minimized these acts as mere reactions to her own aggressive behavior, which she told me, had increased, over time, since she left her first abuser. Cathy was a high school graduate and had been gainfully employed, most of the time, for over nineteen years. Cathy told me that her father was a verbally abusive alcoholic, but described her mother and siblings as very strong and loving. She related no physical or sexual childhood abuse. Cathy had two children and, at the time I interviewed her was living with a friend, while she and her partner looked for an apartment.

CHRISTINE was a 32 year old Caucasian female, survivor who had left her abusive mate three years before we talked. She had not been abused or beaten by another man, since then, and was happily remarried. She was a high school graduate, and had been gainfully employed sporadically throughout her adult life. Christine also described her childhood as happy, and reported no abuse or victimization during that time. She lived with her husband, her daughter, and her new infant son, and described herself as a housewife.

DEVERA was a 51 year old, an African-American, female, survivor, who had fled from her extremely abusive mate 5 years before. Since then, she had never been abused or beaten by a man again. She would receive her Bachelors Degree, later that year, and planned to go on for her Ph.D. Devera had been gainfully employed for 25 years, but had become permanently disabled for 5 years prior to our interview, as a direct and nearly fatal result of her ex-husband's abuse. She described her childhood as idyllic, and reported no experience of childhood abuse or victimization. She lived alone, with extended visits from an adult sibling who sometimes rented a room from her, and enjoyed a large circle of family and friends. She was very proud of her adult son and daughter, and of her grandchild, all of whom she was very close to.

DOROTHY was a 55 year old, African-American, female survivor, who had left her first abusive mate 40 years before our interview. She had experienced multiple abusive relationships with men since then, however she had not been beaten by a domestic partner for 21 years, at the time we talked. Dorothy had been gainfully employed for 25 years, but had later become disabled from gainful employment due to her numerous medical problems. Some of these were directly related to her prior abuse. Dorothy had not completed high school due to her learning disabilities. Dorothy had also experienced childhood abuse and victimization. She was the mother of two adult children, a son, and a daughter. At the time I met with her, she was homeless, and in immediate need of emergency money for food and personal items .

ELLEN was a 49 year old, Caucasian, female, survivor, who had left her abusive mate 19 years before our interviews. She was proud to say that she had never beaten or abused by a man again. She did remarry once, after she left, and then, become divorced again. At the time we talked, Ellen was renting a room, and living alone. She shared a good relationship with her non-abusive boyfriend of 5 years, but did not think that she would ever get married again. Ellen had engaged in gainful employment for her entire life, frequently working two jobs, at the same time. Her most recent job position was as a rape victim advocate. She was a high school graduate, but was also very knowledgeable in several areas, and presented herself with confidence. Although Ellen was emotionally and physically abused by her mother, she did not experience any childhood sexual abuse. She had two children, whom she had not seen, for a period of 19 years, since her abusive ex-husband gained custody of them.

JANICE was a 44 year old Caucasian, female, survivor, who had left her first abusive husband twenty years before we talked. After she left him, she later, married another man, who was also mentally abusive, and she eventually divorced him. Janice had not been beaten, or abused, by a domestic partner for 8 years. Janice had been gainfully employed for over 20 years, but had recently become disabled from work due to several psychological and physical problems; many of these, she believed, were directly related to her prior abuse. Janice had a high school education. She had also experienced childhood abuse and victimization, like several of the other survivors that I interviewed. She was the mother of an adult son and of a fifteen year old daughter, who did not live with her. Janice was renting a one bedroom apartment, in which she lived alone.

LAURIE was a 33 year old, Caucasian, female, survivor, who had left her first abusive mate 12 years before we met. After leaving him, she went on to be beaten and abused by two more husbands. She had not been beaten by a domestic partner for almost a year, at the time we talked. However, she had been facing great difficulties in gaining protection and safety, along with adequate material and emotional support. Laurie had no substantial work history, due to the past domination and control exerted by her former mates. She had attended community college, before she met her first abuser. Laurie had also experienced childhood abuse and victimization. Laurie was living at a homeless shelter with her three children when I interviewed her.

LINDA was a 37 year old, Latina, female, survivor, who had left her abusive mate 12 years before we talked. Linda had not been beaten or abused by a man for 8 years. Although Linda was physically disabled, and often confined to a wheelchair, she still engaged in gainful employment, sporadically. Linda was a high school graduate and she enjoyed doing regular volunteer work. She described her family of origin as loving and supportive, and she related no incidents of childhood sexual or physical abuse. She was living with her two children, along with her parents in their family home. Linda was also helping her father take care of her disabled mother.

MARY ANN was a 55 year old, Caucasian, female, survivor, who had left her first abusive husband 29 years before our interviews. She had experienced multiple abusive relationships with men during her life, but had not been beaten by a domestic partner for over 5 years, at the time we talked. Mary Ann was proud to say that she had been gainfully employed for 35 years, but had recently become disabled from gainful employment due to psychological and physical disabilities that were directly related to her prior abuse. Mary Ann had had completed over 80 lower division college units, but was having difficulty completing the mathematics requirements for her Associate of Science degree. Mary Ann had also experienced childhood physical, emotional, and sexual abuse from several perpetrators. She was the mother of two adult sons and was very proud of her five grandchildren. Mary Ann lived alone.

MICHELLE was a 39 year old, Caucasian, female, survivor, who had left her abusive mate 19 years before we talked. She had been in one long-term relationship with a man, since, which eventually ended due to reasons that did not involve domestic abuse. Michelle had been gainfully employed for 20 years. She described her family of origin as very supportive and loving, and she reported no childhood physical or sexual abuse. Michelle had a high school education and had completed a trade school program. Michelle had an adult daughter, who was happily married, and living independently; she had a seventeen year old daughter, who was living in her home, at the time of our interview.

RACHEL was a 32 year old, Latina, female, survivor, who had left her abusive mate 13 years before we talked. She was proud to tell me that, since she left him, she had never been beaten or abused again. She shared, what she described, as a happy relationship, living with her current boyfriend of 10 years; they planned to get married the following year. Rachel had engaged in gainful employment for most of her life and was, at the time, assisting her fiancé with his business. She would be completing her GED in the near future. Although, Rachel was emotionally abused by her adoptive mother as a child, she had never experienced childhood physical or sexual abuse. She had two children who lived with her and her devoted partner.

ROSE was a 39 year old Caucasian, female survivor, who left her abusive mate 14 years before I interviewed her. She later remarried, and had recently realized that her new relationship had also become mentally and physically abusive. Rose had been gainfully employed for most of the time for 19 years. She had been physically, sexually, and emotionally abused during her childhood by more than one immediate family member. She later lost custody of her children to her first abusive mate at the time they divorced. Last year, she attempted to return to college, but was unable to do so because of her abuser's persistent threats. She was preparing to flee the country at the time I interviewed her. Rose had two children, who still were living with her abusive ex- husband.

VERONICA was a 36 year old, Latina, female, survivor, who had left her abusive husband 5 years before I talked to her. She had been remarried for 3 years to her recent partner, a man whom she described as non-violent. Although, they were having financial and housing difficulties, she described her relationship as happy. Veronica had engaged in gainful employment, most of the time, for over 16 years. She had also finished her Associate Degree, and hoped to go on for her Bachelor's Degree. She described her family of origin as loving and supportive, and related no incidents of childhood sexual, or physical victimization. She was living with her husband and her three children in an apartment, adjacent to her parents and to her brother's home.

YVONNE was a 45 year old, Latina, female, who had left her first abusive mate 20 years before we talked. She later married another man, who also abused and beat her. Her third ex-husband was verbally, but not physically abusive. She was single at the time I interviewed her, and had not been beaten again by a domestic partner again. She was disabled, at the time, due to serious medical and emotional issues; she was a three year cancer survivor. She was very close to completing her Bachelor's Degree, but was having great difficulty because of medical problems; these were compounded by her persistent, long-term learning disabilities. Yvonne had experienced childhood abuse and victimization. However, she also expressed the extreme pain she experienced, as a child, because of anti-Mexican verbal slurs she heard, while walking to school, from the whites in her community. She was the mother of three adult children, and of a ten year old son. She lived with her minor child, along with one of her adult children.

THE INTERVIEW SESSIONS

During our interview sessions, I explored the relationship between the survivor's own personal experience, her self-evaluation, and her ongoing efforts to problem solve, avoid future abuse and to reclaim her life. They also talked about the role of formal and informal support systems in their long-term experience. In Part 2 which follows, prior findings from experts intermingle and are enhanced by the experience and insights of survivors. Several recommendations from the survivors themselves were also explored in order that domestic violence survivors can, hopefully, be better informed in the future about the challenges, they will face, Family members, friends and service providers can also better understand how to help victims and survivors. To this end, both provider efforts, and domestic violence funds can be better directed at those issues that are most crucial to those who want to end the cycle of family violence, over the long term.

PART TWO

TALKING TO
LONG TERM SURVIVORS

FROM NOW ON

I will not dwell in the anger of yesterday,
nor get lost in memories of what I despair,
I will not sit in the shadows of darkness,
For nothing is found to benefit me there.

I will not be held prisoner by foolish pride,
afraid of others and what they think they see.
I will not quietly wait for another's answers,
but I will question and search till I am free,

I will not be a victim of someone else's shame,
letting indifference take away from what I have to give.
I will not be buried in pits of excuses and doubts

I will test cleansing waters of change . . .
I will grow and I will live.

by Lee Michael

from her book, "I Started To Say 'I Love You' But Your
Fist Got In The Way And Other Love Poems"
©Quinn Publishing, Las Vegas 1994

CHAPTER FOUR

SURVIVORS TALK ABOUT STAYING OUT
BETWEEN TWO WORLDS

The collective experience of the long term survivors I interviewed reaffirmed my own experience that life, after leaving an abuser is challenging, often very difficult and sometimes very painful. Survival involved struggle, hard work, problem-solving and learning to adapt to new, sometimes unfamiliar social environments. She may suffer from terror, shame disorientation, confusion, a sense of worthlessness, failure, and a loss of social identity after leaving (Bowker 1993). These feelings can continue to persist as she begins her new life. Survivors can also experience an overwhelming sense of alienation, a loss of power, or a general disaffiliation from the larger social system. This has been described by some as a feeling of "everything falling apart" - a "liminal state" of being "in-between two worlds", a journey of uneasy and often turbulent transition (Bard 1994). During this time the survivor may even feel alienated from herself Herman 1997) and be especially vulnerable to returning to an environment that may have been abusive, but at least is familiar to her. She may even feel protected from others or from her fear of the unknown by going back to her abuser, even though he has harmed her emotionally and/or physically many times in the past.

The women I interviewed expressed similar feelings. They had to begin the process of redefining and reevaluating themselves - to identify themselves as survivors, instead of as victims in order to "stay away". They needed to create new goals, new solutions, and new relationships in order to resist the temptation of returning to their old destructive patterns. They needed to increase their self-worth and sense of empowerment in the "new world" they now inhabited. During this adaptive process, most of the women I talked to had managed to gain a new, improved, positive evaluation of themselves. Yet, in spite of this, they all agreed that the process of healing, and rebuilding their new lives was still not

29

complete. Instead, it was constantly unfolding for them in various ways. When one problem was solved, there was always a new obstacle or challenge to encounter. When one set of goals was achieved, new goals had to be created.

GOAL ORIENTED BEHAVIOR

After taking a close look at the collective information obtained from our interview sessions, I was able to classify into five goal-oriented categories those mindsets that every long term survivor thought were essential to have, or to develop in order to gain and maintain the ability to "stay out" of abusive relationships.

1. Gaining Positive Self Evaluation

2. Learning Effective Problem Solving

3. Avoiding Potential Abusers

4. Having a Higher Quality of Life.

5. Gaining Social Connection and Support

GOAL ONE

Positive Self-Evaluation

In a recent autobiography, one survivor of spousal abuse related the devastating effects her husband's abuse had rendered on her assumptions about "home" and, even more importantly, about herself. Michelle Weldon in her 1999 book, "I Closed My Eyes: Revelations of a Battered Woman," beautifully described the very negative impact on self esteem that many survivors experience,

> "Surviving domestic violence is like walking away from a raging fire that has consumed your home, your life, and your self-definition. You are plagued with the details of how this atrocious fire began, how it spread and how it took so long for you to jump to safety" (1999:xi).

Many of the long term survivors I talked to had similar thoughts and experiences. They expressed how dramatically their self-image had deteriorated while with their abusers. Some women spent months after they left, simply trying to better understand and evaluate what had actually happened to them: why they had changed and why it had happened. Had they deserved this, some-how? Had they brought it upon themselves? Some women said they had not valued themselves highly enough or had expected too little from others. Many felt they needed to redefine themselves as women and to evaluate themselves in a more positive manner: to develop a better self image, know themselves better, gain self-realization, increase self-esteem, and truly accept themselves. Most survivors agreed that this new, improved sense of self was not easy to gain, even though the abuser was no longer criticizing them or putting them down and no longer living in their house-hold. For instance, Rachel, who had been gone 13 years from her abuser, said it had taken her a very long time to become what she called a "real" survivor. She had lost so much of herself when with him, that she had to reclaim her "entire identity "after she left. Another survivor, Dorothy, said it also took her a very long time to value herself more highly or, in her words, to begin to "love herself",

> "My situation was within me. You see, I had to learn to accept myself - I'm going to tell you, the hardest part - I had to learn to love ME - for myself. You know I was always the type of person wondering, 'Oh, do they like me? Do so and so like me?' - or I was always trying to put on the show, or make an impression to someone - like selling myself, like a telemarketer, or something … Just to make them like me."

Cassandra, who was attending graduate school when we talked, explained that surviving abuse, to her meant making an effort to develop a different mindset and a new self image:

> "A victim - you're still … you may be away from the re-lationship but you're still mentally bound to that rela-tionship. A survivor - you not only physically, mentally,

31

> and emotionally left the abusive relationship ... You
> know what happened and of course you can't forget it!
> But *you don't dwell on it.* You don't feel like 'Well, I'm
> always going to be this kind of person. I'm always going
> to be an abused person.' You don't keep that kind of ac-
> tivity going on in your mind."

Several other survivors agreed that this process of redefinition
and reevaluation can take a long time, that sometimes there is no
"quick fix". Two women said they did not become "real survivors" until a very long time *after* they left. Mary Ann, who was
55 years old when we talked, regretted the many years she had
continued to spend in relationships with abusive men even after
she left her first husband, when he brutally beat her as a young
bride and permanently injured her back. She said she "didn't really become a survivor" until fifteen years after that. For her, it
would require five years of sobriety, intensive therapy, and finally
getting back in college again,

> "When I first started school that was who I was - I was
> still a victim. But then, I realized that a victim wasn't
> who I was - that was just things that happened to me. I
> knew I had felt better, but it hadn't occurred to me that
> I had changed that much. The first time I was definitely
> a victim and I was going to about two or three A.A.
> meetings a day - seven days a week at that time and I
> was getting counseling ... and AA was giving me recov-
> ery and comfort from the program - and somewhere
> along the line - I became a survivor rather than a vic-
> tim."

GOAL TWO

Effective Problem Solving

When long term survivors talked to me about ending the abuse in
their lives, they often mentioned learning to become more effective problem solvers and better decision makers. Survivors also
emphasized the importance of learning new ways to handle vari

ous difficulties they faced in everyday life. Some survivors said this meant taking responsibility for their own problems. Others thought it meant taking direct action, even being aggressive, and taking the initiative right away against any obstacle they encountered. "Victims" in comparison, were thought of as being passive and not taking the actions necessary, when they should. A victim, according to women, tended to rely on others, or to behave in a "helpless" manner. A survivor, in contrast, relied on "herself". Effective problem solving was seen as one way of preventing "past mistakes" and as a way to foster future happiness, independence, and autonomy. Some survivors expressed the need for developing more "mental strength" and changing their approach to problems. One survivor, Janice, articulated to me a common sentiment among many survivors, and even among the general public,

> "A victim wears her abuse - refuses to do anything
> about it. A survivor - she helps herself!"

Another survivor, Linda, also stressed the importance of a survivor having self-reliance, and never being dependent upon others to solve her problems for her,

> "You have to be the one who pulls yourself out of
> that situation - only you, not someone else!"

Mary Ann believed that a survivor's problem-solving abilities - or lack thereof were affected by her self-image. According to her, low self-esteem played a crucial role in good decision making because many victims, like her, have negative self images,

> "They don't do what deep down they know they need to
> do. A victim lets things happen to them. Even though
> they may fight back on the surface, and they think they
> are trying really hard to change and avert problems,
> physical or emotional, they are not really in their deep-
> est heart averting the problems ... it's because down
> deep they feel like all this stuff just happens to them be-
> cause they are bad, and therefore they must deserve it."

Cassandra also said that a survivor's self-evaluation was closely related to what actions she decided to take or not take. She emphasized the importance of a survivor increasing her self-understanding. She had learned after leaving her abuser, that "knowing herself", and what she wanted in life, enabled her to take the steps necessary to pursue her goals,

> "I would say you have to be secure in yourself [to be a survivor]. You have to know who you are and what you are - and once you know that, you know what you are capable of. You know what you can handle and what you can't handle - you know what you want - and then you go after it."

Cassandra suggested that survivors might even be able to benefit from memories of their past abuse, by thinking about what had happened to them in a positive, proactive way. She thought that even bad experiences could be good as long as people used them to learn and to gain more motivation and strength to pursue their goals.

> If you were able to go through all of that physical and mental stress with that person - if he put you through that - and you survived, then you can push yourself through some other status that is going to have you mentally and physically pushing yourself. And then - whatever levels you want to go to - you can make it."

While the survivors above emphatically expressed the importance of taking action, others felt more cautious about acting too quickly. They were actually making purposeful, studied efforts to avoid impulsive decision making. They were critical of themselves for acting too quickly in the past, especially in regard to relationships with men. Mary Ann, for example, said that being a survivor, for her, meant learning new ways to *think first* and to *halt* her prior tendency to act on impulse. She said that action "without thinking", had caused her to make many, many mistakes in the past,

"Being a survivor doesn't stop things from happening to

you - it makes you look at them differently - it's how you deal with things that happen - rather than just allowing them to happen. People start thinking things out a little more, considering consequences."

Mary Ann stated that her problem-solving had greatly improved because of her A.A. recovery group. There she had enjoyed the opportunity of meeting other people who shared similar experiences with her. Her A. A. membership had actually been a major turning point in her life,

"When you go to AA, you talk about what is bothering you that affects your sobriety and then other people will say, "When I had a hard time staying sober, I did such and such and it worked for me", and you ... it kind of goes around the table ... and they make suggestions - not for what they want you to do, but what *they* did and you can kind of pick and choose and listen to each person's story and take what you think will work for you. It's kind of like a trial and error thing. You try this, and if it doesn't work, you try that ... [T]hat was the beginning of me being able to think more clearly and to recognize them - the abusers ..."

GOAL THREE

Avoiding Abusers

All of the long term survivors I interviewed stated that being a survivor, definitely meant not getting into an abusive relationship with a man again. Some survivors had experienced, one or more violent relationships, since they fled their first abusive mates. Yet, despite these unfortunate episodes, *none of* these women had been in what *they termed* an abusive relationship for a period of at least three years at the time we talked (the three year time period, as you may recall, was in conformity to my initial research definition of a "survivor" and "exit") In fact, many of the survivors had become extremely guarded around men and had postponed beginning any new relationship. According to these women, caution was essential, even if a new partner promised them protection, financial assistance, comfort, or companionship. Yvonne, said that, since she had become stronger, she was, convinced that her safety and well-being, itself, depended on making sure she avoided the temptation to be with a man again,

> "How can I say it … I feel I'm surviving because I don't allow myself to fall back into a "hard-up-ness" - like saying, "Oh I'm going to be with a man because I need a man and, whether he abuses me or not, or I need the money so bad I'm going to go with this guy …"

Avoiding an abusive relationship, for Yvonne meant beginning to learn ways to recognize a potentially abusive suitor, *even before they became involved with him.* One survivor described for me, her newly found, carefully studied confidence in her ability to "tell" if a man was dangerous, or if he could possibly become abusive,

> "What I have found out is that some men have that power over some women. Now I recognize it – I know it for what it is, and I can deal with it. I never saw it before, but boy can I see it now. I can tell."

When another survivor, Devera was asked how she could tell if a man was going to be abusive, she explained,

> "Oh there's inflections in his voice - there's a way that he looks at you, especially when he's trying to get next to you. His tone of voice, the way he talks, and the way he looks - and he knows exactly the right buttons to push, at the exact right moment - to break you down. He knows how to manipulate a situation around to his favor, no matter what, because it's never his fault - But, you see - I recognize that now - and I've learned to manipulate it - *back to what it is!"*

Mary Ann said that she, too, like Devera, had gained the ability to recognize a man who might possibly abusive. Once more, she credited years of therapy, as well as her involvement in twelve-step recovery groups, for her newly found skills,

> "I used to sit in AA meetings and I would watch their eyes ... and once I realized [that] I could do it - every guy I met I did that to, immediately ... and it was like, nope - I don't care how good looking he is or how sexy he is - he's got those eyes - screw it! The look in their eyes - it's something almost intangible - it's ... ah ... sneaky ... kind of sneaky, sly, slick, hip slick and cool - you know, that kind of thing. And they're always very self absorbed with the attitude of "Yeah, I'll help you get this, but what am I going to get out of it?" I've gotten involved with a few that kind of slid by - but now, I can usually tell ... and I can look at a man in the eyes now and I can tell you if he's violent. I can see it, in a heartbeat, and it's like, 'I don't care" - he can be the best looking guy on the face of the earth - and have a million bucks and I say, 'Tough - get away from me', because I can see it now. But, then - I couldn't see it, at that point."

Mary Ann articulated for me how her skills had developed. She had managed to sharpen her perceptions about the men she met though a heightened awareness that occurred when she noticed a particular look in a man's eyes, words, or mannerisms that signaled danger to her. These observations had enabled Mary Ann to develop a new mindset about the men she would interact with, inside and outside of her recovery group, and she began to avoid men with certain characteristics, in order to protect her well-being and her new self-image as a survivor. Yvonne also said that she had become very cautious when approached in public by an unfamiliar man. Sometimes, something as simple as the smell of alcohol, or a sudden movement would make her very uneasy. She explained to me that she also had learned to recognize possible abusers, in particular, by watching their drinking habits,

> "I've learned from my past experience. No. No. No. I may like the guy - he may be cute, but I'm not going into put myself in a dangerous situation. No. No. No. No.

Everybody thinks I'm weird. They think I'm crazy, I think, because I won't get with them - I don't. He's cute. Big deal, you know - cuteness over my health and me? No way! I don't need no one [anyone] abusive - no more. No way. I watch mainly if a man likes to drink a lot - but I watch mainly if he's abusive, or if he's real violent, or if he's a "lovey-dovey type" - a calm nice guy. You know - I'll watch for that. And if a guy looks abusive, I'm not even going to bother going out with him the next day. Let's say I'm sitting there, and say, someone asks me to dance, and this guy gets aggressive - like being jealous, showing strong emotions ... No. That's too much of a difference. No. No. I don't like it. I know that something's up. No more. No way!"

Yvonne's experience had caused her, like Mary Ann, to initially back off from a man and to interact very cautiously with him until she had gathered more time to observe his behavior. Her own particular perceptions had become keenly sensitized to the smell of alcohol on a man's breath or clothing and to a man's specific drinking behavior; she was also very sensitive to his level of aggression when he interacted with others. If a man appeared even slightly aggressive, according to Yvonne, he would probably be a potential abuser. In addition, some of the long term survivor I spoke with had become committed to, not only avoiding abusers, but also, to avoiding any sort of romantic relationship with men, at least for a while. Devera told me that she would like to be married someday, but not before she finished her education, and knew even more about herself. She expressed the belief,

"If women knew themselves better, they would stop settling for less power in their lives, due to societal pressure to 'have a man'."

She went on to say that she thought it was important for a victim to become a truly independent women, after leaving, before she even considered getting into any serious relationship with a man,

"I think it's kind of discovering who you are, too, because it's kind of hard to know if someone's like you if you don't know who you are. If I don't know who I am, how am I going to find someone like me? See I've always heard men say, "I've worked too hard to ..." - well this woman has worked too hard to get here to go back for anything. I mess up on my own enough. I don't need anybody to help me do that! I can fall by myself ... that's my driving force ... that I want to see just how well I can do. By myself."

Devera went on to express that she had learned a lot from her struggle as a domestic violence survivor and did not want to repeat her prior mistakes. She wanted me to warn other women that, sometimes, just turning to a man can represent a somewhat simple but extremely deceptive solution,

"I know there is no way I'm going down those highways again ... I'm not burning any bridges - it's just I know that road - I know the pitfalls, I know the bumps - and I know the speed bumps ... I know that road. And I don't want anyone to learn it the way I did! The easy way is to get married again, have somebody to take care of you - and then have that same person beat your ass again. Sometimes they [women] get lucky - but the numbers just aren't for that ..."

USING VIOLENCE IF NECESSARY

Several survivors told me they were willing to use violence, if necessary, in order to protect themselves and not be abused or beaten again. Most said they would use extreme, even deadly violence, if it were necessary, should they ever be attacked again. For some women, this meant physically defending themselves, but for other survivors, it meant even more. When asked what would happen if they were ever attacked again by a man, nearly every survivor expressed tremendous anger. Some women had already rehearsed what their reaction to a potential assault would be, and had thought of various strategies, ahead of time, they would use to protect themselves. Betty, who used to be terrified of her ex-husband, told me that she would now be able to defend herself against him, or against any man, if he ever became violent with her,

> "I have a baseball bat. I ain't gonna' worry about nothing - somebody's getting knocked the fuck out. 'Cause I am not taking no more ass-whuppins'. No. Hell no. This year - No! It's a new millennium. I'll take them out! There ain't no way in the world. No! Uh-Uh! I have too much to live for these days. Hell No!"

Yvonne became emotional and very agitated when she shared with me what she would do if she were ever beaten again. She told me that calling the police, along with physically defending herself, might be a solution, but it was clear, as Yvonne continued to speak, that her reaction might be more extreme,

> "He would be sorry, because I would not tolerate - there's no damn way. I must be an idiot … and if they say they're going to kill me - better kill me now, because I will not accept that. Oh, he would be sorry. I would put a stick over his head or some object and say, "Get the hell out of here" … or "I'm calling the cops on you" … Oh, just the thought of it really pisses me off. It angers me - just the thought of it. Just the conversation of anyone laying a finger on me. I don't think so. I mean it. I would flip. I would physically flip."

Ellen had not been beaten by anyone for over 19 years when we talked, but regretfully, had lost custody of her children due to her abuser's impressive financial assets and social connections. She was initially very guarded when I asked what her reaction to any future attempt at violence against her might be. Yet, as Ellen began to reply, the depth of her rage at even the possibility of ever being abused by a man again began to emerge and heighten,

> "Oh God, I would probably … I would like to think that I would do everything the way you supposedly should do

it. I would seek shelter - I would call the police - I would go through the horrendous business of doing whatever they wanted me to do. I'd go through whatever forensics I had to go through to provide evidence of the abuse - of the being photographed for bruises and all that type thing. But there is a part of me that would kill him. Right there on the spot – 'BOOM - BOOM - BOOM! You had it!' Throw him in the pool and drown him! I truly think there is a part of me that would just want to castrate him! 'Honey, let me drive the car over you, and then I'm going to back it up, back and forth, two or three times just to make sure you're flat!'

GOAL FOUR

An Improved Quality Of Life

According to long term survivors, having an improved or higher quality of life was characterized in three major ways. A better life to them meant having in their new day to day experiences as women the following characteristics:

- A SENSE OF NORMALCY

- A SENSE OF RECOVERY

- A SENSE OF MASTERY

NORMALCY

For many survivors, a sense of *normalcy* meant finally being able to perceive of and refer to others of their lives and relationships as "being "normal". Being "normal" was described by survivors as having "nice", "regular" relationships with friends, doing the "everyday things" that they used to do, or engaging in activities they saw what they called "normal" people doing. It was also described as having a "normal" man as a husband or partner. "Being normal" was further described by survivors as being able to go shopping and to visit friends when they wanted to. Betty, who was, at the time happily married to her new husband, smiled as she said,

> "I mean - I can actually wake up in the morning and smile about something. You know I was able after a while to go to work and do things - and, you know, now I can - I can just live ... I can do what I've got to do - and friends come over, and ... you know ..."

RECOVERY

Having a higher quality of life was also described by some survivors in terms of *"recovery"*. Recovery, for these women, meant being clean and sober and actively involved in a recovery program such as A.A. or N.A. Those who emphasized the importance of recovery also believed that not using drugs or alcohol, made them better able to avoid being victimized again by anyone, in particular, by men. Not being abused meant, not only leaving their batterers, but also, ending their own self-abuse, through recovery, from destructive drug or alcohol addictions. Ellen described the improved quality of life she was enjoying, at the time, not only because she had left her abuser, but also because she had finally stopped drinking. She admitted to me that her alcoholism had developed as a coping mechanism when her husband used to beat her. The process of coming to grips with her addiction didn't culminate, for Ellen, until nearly seventeen years after her divorce,

> "I mean I'm really and truly alive. I'm not living on a ... I'm not drugged. I'm not living 'out of it.' I'm really, truly alive, living each experience as it comes up. For the first time in my life, I am really truly taking care of myself! I am taking care of me and everything else is falling in behind. That's the first time in my life I have put myself first! I joined the athletic club - "ritzy" - top of the line. And I've been constantly growing and stretching - and growing and stretching - and growing and stretching - going through all of these wonderful self improvement things and saying, 'Yes, I want to do this -

I am worthy of this,' and not giving it a second thought, just doing it because it has to be done."

NOTE: Although, some survivors thought that their prior use of alcohol or drugs had, perhaps, increased their vulnerability to being abused, they still did not consider their addictions to be any justification for being beaten, or abused, by their partners.

MASTERY

Long term survivors also described having a better quality of life in terms of *mastery*. Having a sense of mastery meant engaging in self-improvement, setting and achieving goals, having a sense of accomplishment, and enjoying a feeling of success. Sometimes a survivor would describe achievement in terms of how those in her present and future social world would evaluate her. Devera told me that she was pursuing her post-graduate degree, not only, "for herself", but to guarantee that people would think more highly of her,

> "I don't care if I don't get a degree - part of this is that I am not stupid and I am going to prove that I am not stupid. This is proof positive - husband - anybody else who has told me I'm stupid - "I'm not stupid and here is the proof!" So all those times somebody was calling me stupid - "You stupid ignorant bitch!" Now they'll see me different[ly] ...."

Cassandra spoke of mastery and achievement in a different way – as a battle that she was finally really winning. She was working full time, finishing her Master's Degree, and still finding time to be a loving mother. She also planned to go on for her Ph.D. to achieve her dream of being a C.E.O. She thought of herself not just as a survivor, but as a "Conqueror" who was now totally ready for any new challenge that might be ahead of her,

> "I don't consider myself a survivor - I consider myself a "Conqueror"! Because, not only did I go past a survivor, because the survivor you're - like, 'Whew - I made it through - Whew I didn't know I was gonna' make it

43

through. Okay I can do this better and let me get my life back up.' And you get yourself back to a status quo where, 'I'm happy - I've got my own place - I've got this - I've got a car' You're happy with - I would say 'normal.' But a Conqueror! You decide, 'Okay - that's it! I went through all of that. Yes, I made it through … but there's something even more and I got to get to it!'"

"Turn your wounds into wisdom "

Oprah Winfrey

CHAPTER FIVE

SURVIVORS TALK ABOUT STAYING OUT
SOCIAL SUPPORT & CONNECTION

Survivors spoke at length about the importance of social connection and support over their long-term experience. Many of the women I interviewed had become very socially isolated, during the time they were with their abusers. After leaving, they sometimes experienced loneliness, social isolation, and a feeling of being "cut off" from the "normal" world around them. They expressed the need for communication and support from other people, along with a sense of security and protection, for themselves, and their families. Many needed help from their communities obtaining material provisions for themselves and for their children such as money, food, childcare, medical assistance and housing. Some survivors also faced additional challenges, just *learning how* to gain support from others, while still maintaining their newly- found sense of autonomy, and independence as individuals.

GOAL FIVE

Gaining Social Support & Connection

The need for social support had been articulated several times by experts and domestic violence survivors at large. Surviving abuse cannot be undergone alone - reconnection with others, constitutes the essence of support, assistance and healing (Bowker 1993; Ellis 1992; Goetting 1999; Gondolf and Fisher 1988; Hoff 1990; Herman 1997; Stark and Flitcraft 1998; Walker 1994). Some of the long term survivors I spoke with were able to gain needed assistance from informal sources such as their own family of origin, pseudo-family members, new partners, and friends. Women who were able to obtain predictable assistance from closely connected sources such as these, tended to describe positive outcomes, over the long term. However, for some victims gaining and maintaining social support from informal sources was problematic after they left, when relatives and friends were absent, afraid, unavailable, or unable to understand what was going on. In some cases, friends, or neighbors may have even been sympathetic to the abuser.

Since a domestic violence shelter was utilized by only one of the survivors I interviewed, the majority of women had to rely on institutional sources of protection and support, such as police and government agencies. Gaining support and assistance from police, social service agencies, and courts can be very difficult. Most women stated that, when they turned to these for help, they experienced disappointing outcomes. Negative experiences were common, due to often frustrating interactions with what they perceived as apathetic, uncaring, insufficiently informed workers. Only about 25% of the women I interviewed thought that social service agencies, police, courts, lawyers, governmental and social service agencies were effective sources of support. Recovery groups and mental health services were rated more highly by some survivors, while relationships formed at workplace, and at school were rated very highly as major sources of support.

SOCIAL SUPPORT - BASIC NEEDS

Some of the basic needs long term survivors had, and how they gained and evaluated the *formal* forms of support available for these will first be explored further. What are commonly referred to as *informal* sources of social support such as biological family and surrogate family groups, along with how survivors evaluated these will be explored later.

The basic, immediate needs of survivors are:

- Safety And Protection

- Shelter, Food, Money

- Child Well-Being And Custody

- Medical And Mental Health Issues

Safety & Protection

Leaving an abuser can be a very triumphant event but "getting away" does not automatically offer a woman protection from further abuse (Zorza 1991; Browne 1997; Ellis 1992; Ewing 1997; Gelles 1997; Rosen and Stith 1997). Many survivors remain extremely afraid, sometimes for a very long time after they leave. Domestic violence expert, Lee Bowker (1993) after studying over 1,000 battered women, outlined many of those specific fears. Bowker found that, before leaves, a woman may fear that an unsuccessful escape could lead to worse battering, or to her death. Survivors may also fear that, when they exit, the abuser's retaliation will also be directed at relatives or at close friends. Women also expressed great fear that their children would be harmed emotionally, mentally or physically. Survivors often also felt extremely vulnerable. The fear of future violence or even of her own murder can remain with a survivor, indefinitely, even long after her separation, divorce, or criminal prosecution of the batterer. Even years later, while still in hiding many survivors remain afraid of being found. My own personal experience provides one example. For many years after I left, my terror of being found and killed by him had still not subsided. I would sometimes think I had seen my abuser across the street while shopping and I would frequently dream that he was coming into my room to murder me while I slept

Shelter

After escaping from my own batterer, I was very fortunate to obtain short term protection, from my 30 day stay at a domestic violence shelter. For many women, who leave, a similar hidden location, "safe place" or domestic violence shelter is sought for refuge (Bowker and Mauer 1985; Browne 1997; Loseke 1992). However, studies show that, while battered women's shelters have been often found to be the most effective means of ending the cycle of abuse, they have been actually utilized by a relatively, very small percentage of women who flee their mates (Bowker 1993). This may be due to the fact that shelters are always in short supply (Bard 1994; Bowker and Maurer 1985; Gelles 1997; Sherman 1997). As a result, many women have been forced to turn to other less effective sources of help (Bowker and Maurer 1985, 1986). Domestic violence shelters also cannot guarantee permanent pro-

47

tection. If a woman is fortunate enough to obtain shelter assistance, the typical stay is often very short, and related services may be limited (Dobash and Dobash 1979; Sherman 1997). At the same time, we need only to look at the nightly news, or to open our daily newspapers, to be reminded that battered women and their children have a critical need for these and other forms of short-term, and long-term protection and shelter.

The long term survivors I spoke with all agreed that gaining shelter, safety, and protection for themselves and their children was their primary concerns after they left their abusers. Yet, as was stated earlier, shelter assistance was available and utilized by only one survivor out of these sixteen victims. Some, having left their abusers many years earlier, had not even heard of such a place as a battered women's shelter at the time they fled. Other long term survivors knew about shelters, but had been unwilling to go to one. Most of them admitted that they could have probably benefited from this form of assistance, but stated that domestic violence shelters were unavailable to them at the time they left, short of space, or too restrictive. One woman sought shelter, but could not qualify for lodging because she did not have children with her. Another stated that she was unable to obtain space in a domestic violence shelter because her abuser was "only" psychologically, and not physically abusive. One survivor, who was employed at the time she left, said that the shelter curfews made her ability to keep her evening job impossible, so she was forced to find another solution.

Cassandra, the only survivor in my study fortunate enough to benefit from domestic violence shelter housing and assistance, found it quite helpful, especially since she was later able to combine her shelter stay with material and emotional support from family and friends at her workplace. When she first left her abuser, she took a leave of absence from her job, and then, spent the next thirty days hidden at the shelter. During her stay, she rested, prayed, and attended group therapy sessions. Cassandra believed the peaceful atmosphere at the shelter to have been very helpful at the time because she was also grieving the recent death of her infant child. Still very fearful that her husband might drive by and see her, Cassandra rarely went outside the shelter door, not even to go to the convenience store,

> "I never left the shelter. I was so close to where my ex was, so I said, "I have no reason to be out there." Everything I need is right here. They give you the food; they give you the clothes ... so I had no reason to leave. I was comfortable where I was ... [I]t was a nice amount of time just to relax, especially after having all that stress around me for so long of "I don't want to do this, it may send them off", "I don't want him to hit me", and "You can't do this", "You can't do that", "Make sure this is clean and make sure this is perfect" and it was like - I don't have to make "sure" of anything. Just relax. Calm down - get back to the way life should be."

During her stay at the shelter, Cassandra also devised an extended personal safety plan, which included extending her leave of absence at work further and moving out-of-state temporarily. She also found while she was still at the shelter, while listening to other residents' experiences in group sessions, it was helpful to be able to compare her own experiences with theirs. In group meetings, women collectively supported each other in recovering from, and redefining their abusive experiences. She described to me in detail how, at the shelter, she, along with other survivors empowered themselves as women to begin their new lives,

> "Yeah, it was good because they give you an opportunity to talk about, not so much intimately what you went through, but you have an opportunity to get out the facts of what you were going through as a person and what you were feeling - and how this man was making you feel and how it seemed like every time there was a full moon this person started acting crazy. You have an opportunity to share with other people ... and then you think your situation was bad, but then maybe you hear somebody else's situation who was even worse than yours, - and you think like "Man, you know mine was

bad, but hers was worse!" And then you listen to how long this person had gone through it and how long did I go through it - and then finally all of us came out and said, "That's it - you know we've got to get out!"

Homelessness

Gaining safe, short-term shelter is essential for women and children after they escape, but gaining *and maintaining* adequate, affordable housing is also a major concern, continuing long after women leave. Because of this persistent problem, domestic abuse continues to be one of the leading causes of *homelessness* among women and children in the United States (Salomon and Bassuk 1999; Ollengerger and Moore 1998; Fox 1985; Zorza 1991; Waxman and Hinderliter 1996). Over 50% of the homeless women in the United States are fleeing domestic abuse and cycles of *long-term* homelessness are, often, both initiated *and perpetuated* by the abuse of women (Bard 1994). Gender-specific research of homeless populations has also shown that more homeless women say they have been abused than homeless men (Bassuk 1990).

Police Assistance

Survivors face issues of short-term and sometimes long-term protection especially when very dangerous, possessive or angry mates stalk, or pursue these women and children, sometimes to their death. Some abusers are psychotic or severely obsessed and these men are frequently armed, and unwilling to accept their partner's rejection. One earlier study showed that over 1,400 wives and girlfriends a year were being killed by their partners (Gelles 1997). Many such homicides occur *after* the victim leaves. In fact, women are at greater risk for sub-lethal or lethal violence after leaving and they are 25 times more likely to be victimized by a partner after they separate, than if they remained married (Goetting 1999). Prior findings point to both successes and failures of police and courts in provision of both short and long-term protection for battered women (Berk 1993; Buzawa and Buzawa 1990; Bowker 1993; Ferraro 1999; Fischer and Rose 1995; Sherman, Schmidt and Rogan 1992). I found that many survivors I interviewed had been threatened with lethal violence by their abusers several times. Although they had been encouraged to seek assistance from law enforcement and many of them did so, *only one long term survivor,* Janice said that the police had provided her with a genuine sense of protection and support.

Janice believed that her life may have actually been saved by the concerned policeman who escorted her to an emergency room, waited with her there, and then, explained to physicians that she was being abused by her husband. She was, also, later assisted, by her local police department, to obtain a restraining order. During the days following, patrol officers continued to provide her with a feeling of security and comfort by driving by her apartment frequently and checking up on her. Comparing her experience with the other survivors I spoke with, I couldn't help but wonder if, since Janice was a very attractive, seventeen year old young woman at the time she needed special help, this may have contributed to the extremely protective attitude displayed by law enforcement officers. Unfortunately, even with the assistance of local police, Janice's problems still were not over. Threats and a sense of constant endangerment from her extremely violent ex-husband did not subside. She lived in constant fear of him for many months and still recalled operating her home day care center with all of the curtains drawn for several months. She was terrified that her angry batterer would drive by, and shoot at her and the children playing there through her front windows. He was finally arrested one day during a scheduled child visitation, caught by police, in front of her house with a trunk full of ammunition and guns, and put into prison.

The other survivors I spoke with had been moderately to extremely, disappointed in the assistance they had received from the police. African-American and Latina women expressed their perception of having far less protection from law enforcement when they needed it. The lack of concern and assistance from police officers, experienced by many interviewed may have also been related, in part, to the fact that some of them had left their abusers *before* the current "post O.J." (see Chapter 2) social trend toward increased attention on domestic violence and more police sensitivity took effect. As might be expected, this group of underserved survivors had extremely negative feelings about police attitudes and responses. Betty, who was African American, said she had called police many, times, and they had never helped her. She swore she would never advise an abused woman to rely on the police and added that, in her opinion, a victim should never rely on family members to help either. She expressed her feelings of repeated frustration with law enforcement,

> "Oh, please do not tell them [survivors] to call the police or just to call a family member. The cops would say to me 'Where's your brothers?' And I said 'You got to be sick!' The police - they would take forever and then by that time - like I said - I had to pick up butcher knives, or whatever else and stuff and he'd be done chased out or whatever - and after that I'd call ... I called one of my brothers one time and that was the last time I ever called him to help me. He took *two* hours to come! Oh, please do not tell them to just call the police ... all those little things that make you feel like you're stupid. Don't brush them off and give them that bullshit line ..."

Even though Laurie was Caucasian, she also shared the same frustrations with law enforcement. A few years before we talked, she had been hospitalized, for three days, with a major concussion and head lacerations, due to one of many violent altercations with her ex-husband. He had thrown her on top of a plate glass coffee table in a drunken rage. When Laurie was released from the hospital, the first person she saw, outside, was her abusive husband, waiting for her on the sidewalk. She still recalled the shame she experienced as two policemen that were standing nearby, laughed as they watched as her abuser pull her by her hair down the street. Laurie no longer trusted law enforcement, and she questioned the, seemingly callous, behavior sometimes displayed by police,

> "I'm grateful to the one cop who finally arrested him, after I started screaming, but why did they have to stand there and laugh at me like that?"

Courts And Legal Assistance

Survivors often expressed the need for legal assistance in obtaining court judgments or protective orders. However, unfortunately, many women have found that courts often fail to actually protect them and that restraining orders are frequently ineffective. In fact, many battered wives have been killed while holding protective orders in their hands (Statman 1990). As mentioned earlier, some abusers are dangerously psychotic, armed and completely unwilling to abide by the law. Some may be suicidal. Assistance with long-term hiding, along with identity protection and restoration, in some cases, is needed by many survivors after they leave. Although some of the long term survivors I spoke with, had sought out legal assistance for divorce proceedings, child custody issues and/or to obtain restraining orders, most of them stated they had experienced less assistance from attorneys, judges, and other representatives of the legal and judicial system than they had anticipated. Three survivors found their lawyers satisfactory during their divorce and child custody litigation, but did not consider them meaningful sources of support.

Most survivors said that the legal assistance they were actually able to obtain was far too limited and they attributed this scarcity to their lack of financial resources. Three survivors stated that, even the smaller costs of filing legal documents *pro bono*, by using "self-help" methods, were prohibitive, when they attempted to do so. Four women added that free or sliding-scale legal advice, was either unavailable, had a long waiting list or was insufficient. Some survivors did manage to obtain restraining orders and two survivors had started to do so but didn't follow through with the process. Two survivors had started to press charges on their abusers, but only one of them, Rose, had followed through.

Child Protection, Custody & Support

As we have seen, survivors of domestic abuse also have child protection and custody problems after fleeing their mates (Deed 1991; Liss and Stahly 1993; Wilson 1998; Zorza 1995). Some abusers had actually initiated custody or visitation battles in order to seek revenge on their victims, to further control them, or to remain informed of their whereabouts. An abuser may also have more financial resources and a wider social network than his victim has and manage to actually win custody of the children, not because he is the better parent, but because he can afford a better attorney. Additionally, in what has been referred to as a "new perverse trend" of gender bias among some judges, abusers have sometimes been granted child custody, simply because a woman complained during a court hearing of having been beaten by him (Winner 1996:131). New laws have been introduced to address this very important and often volatile issue of child custody and visitation rights in cases that involve domestic violence, but the resolution of these issues still depends frequently on the perspective or whim of each individual judge. And unfortunately, judges, lawyers, police, and social workers sometimes do make errors and this can open the door to child abduction by an estranged husband or to the further abuse of the woman and her children.

Added to child custody issues facing the long term survivor, are problems of inadequate or non-existent child support. Her increased financial obligations, sometimes compounded by personal factors such as disability, lack of training, insufficient child care and/or low wages can make some mothers reliant on the welfare system. This can lead to demands placed on survivors by district attorneys who want her to provide additional information about the absent father (the abuser) in order to force him to provide child support payments. These consequences may be unwanted or feared by some women due to apprehension about being found by the abuser (Kurz 1998). These aggressive attempts by social services and district attorneys to "find the father" can present a real threat to the survivor's safety. The constant perception of being in danger yet, at the same time, being under undue pressure to comply with child support welfare regulations in order to maintain benefits or child custody, can greatly threaten her own, as well as her children's, sense of well being. I remember when I fled my very violent abuser, receiving those intimidating letters after I applied for welfare benefits. More than once, I was forced to respond and go to hearings in order to fight just for my right to remain safe, alive and to protect my children. I would be sick for two months, each time this pressure reoccurred from worrying that I might lose and have to help locate him.

Rose, who had been anxious for years, told me that her experience with the court system had been very frustrating and disheartening. An ongoing battle with her abuser and then with the legal system, had begun for her over 14 years before we spoke. Her husband had gained custody of their two children after the divorce, and she was ordered to pay a generous amount of monthly child support to him. These payments were strictly enforced, even though, she had never been able to earn, even close to the amount of money her abuser earned. The year before I met her, Rose had tried to reduce her monthly child support payments, so that she could return to college in the hopes of eventually increasing her earning power. Because of her request, her ex husband came to her home and severely beat her, while her new husband was at work. Rose received emergency room treatment for her injuries, and attempted to press charges on her ex husband but she was unable to provide any eyewitnesses to his merciless beating when the case went to court. Her ex-husband appeared at the hearing, surrounded by his friends and some character witnesses, including one prominent community member, who provided a fabricated alibi for his whereabouts at the time of the offense. As a result, Rose lost the case.

Rose had recently become more frightened of her ex husband, than she had ever been before. Making matters worse, her *new* husband was starting to become more and more verbally abusive of her. Rose told me that she was preparing to leave the United States, never to return. She would miss seeing her children, but she really had no other choice. In her opinion, the American court system only worked for those with money. Ellen, another survivor said she had also fought very hard to maintain custody of her children when she left her abusive husband. Despite this, she, too, lost her children, due to her own lack of money and legal resources. As with Rose, the ongoing custody battle had become for Ellen, very stressful, exhausting, and fraught with injustices,

It's so unfair. Of course, the lawyers want a big retainer. I didn't have that kind of money and didn't have the strength, the fiber to fight these people - really, really, truly, didn't have the money. One attorney wanted a $25,000 retainer - I've never had that kind of money in my life. Never will. I've always lived paycheck to paycheck ... and every time I get a nickel ahead, somebody needs a dime of it for some reason. And you call attorneys and you're told you have to keep a log of every time you call, every time you write, what you've gotten from them - what was said by the other person on the phone. I did that for awhile and it got to where I got tired of writing, 'He said fuck you' and she said 'You're crazy' and you go back and read it and you say, 'I don't want anybody to see this! They're going to think there is something *way* wrong with me. I've got to stop doing this ... '"

Laurie, who had already lost custody of her four children to her abuser, also, told me she was very angry at the legal system because the judges and courts always seemed to favor her husband. Like Ellen, she thought this was likely the result of his wealth and higher status in the community. She expressed the terror she always experienced every time she went to court against him, due to his past record of rage and extreme violence every time they had a custody hearing. She told me about two incidents, during which her ex-husband had threatened her, both before and after, the court hearings. Once, he had even chased her down the hallway, outside the courtroom. Laurie expressed the pain and the feeling of social injustice she felt because of her experiences in the court

> "I never realized just how threatened I was by my husband's money - I just loved him so much for so long ... I only get two days to see my 6 year old daughter now - and now they've changed courtrooms on me again! Out here, they care about my daughter mainly because my ex has money and they know him around the community. Welfare mothers like me get sent to the Commissioner and Judge Miller takes the 'paying cases.'"

Mental Health Providers

Some survivors expressed the belief that psychiatrists, counselors, or other mental health providers had provided them with support and healing. Professional or paraprofessional assistance can sometimes becomes necessary for a survivor because her cognitive mental processes can be seriously affected by the overwhelming emotions that continue to rage within her, after she leaves. Families are often forced to leave behind, beloved friends, neighbors, pets, schools, workplace, and church communities. Grief may even be felt by the survivor and her children due to loss of relationship with the abuser (Browne 1997; 1992; Landerburger 1989; Rosen and Stith 1997). Children are often upset by the disruption of their family life. They may also exhibit emotional and behavioral problems from, either witnessing, or being the victims, themselves, of abuse and violence. Mental and emotional problems resulting from these experiences can persist into adulthood. Eleven long term survivors had received therapy for themselves or for their children, at one time or another after they left their abusers. Of these, six women said that their therapists had been a source of major support. Five survivors stated that they were still in therapy, due to either persistent symptoms of depression, or post traumatic stress disorder. Mental health services and therapists were very helpful to several women, especially those who lacked other forms of support in their lives. In stark contrast, a smaller group of survivors were unwilling to rely heavily on therapy fearing they would probably just become overmedicated or just be "telling their problems to a stranger". Yvonne thought that therapists "only pretend to listen",

> "To me, if counseling helps for that person great - but, most of the time, I think you have to go through it, mentally, and figure it out - sometimes by yourself. I don't know - I'm a weak person but I feel I did most of it on my own. Those programs - I don't give them credit because they don't even help. When some people get help out of it - yeah - depending [on] if you have a good counselor. But that's hard to find a good person who will listen and will really, really be there ... some people, its like, 'Oh yeah, oh yeah'. They just 'play it off', you know."

Betty, who was attending family therapy sessions with her children, at the time we talked, said she had hesitated, at first, to seek out professional help, attributing her reluctance to her "strong" self-image. She had always seen herself as being a strong African-American woman, and in order to not "seem weak", she said that she had always avoided talking to a therapist,

> "Now that I think about it, it probably would have helped me earlier if I would have gone and got counseling and stuff or something. It was like ... I didn't know anything about mental health back then. I'm supposed to be a "black strong person" here. I can't go weeping, you know, so I walked around, like in a 'zombie stage' for a long, long time. "

When a survivor experienced a perception of support and help from mental health services, it appeared to be measured in direct relationship to the quality of her interaction with a specific care provider. If the therapist listened well, was open and shared common thoughts and feelings with the survivor and *above all - was not perceived of as judgmental,* he or she was evaluated very highly. Most survivors were extremely sensitive to judgment or criticism from others, and this included the therapists they sought out. Ellen was not very satisfied with the first therapist she went to, but her employer helped her find a therapist that she liked much better. She emphasized the importance of not feeling judged, being taken seriously, and of being *really listened to,*

> "I think she helped me   She certainly helped me get through the last of getting over my anger toward family members - the ex husband and everything. She never belittles my concerns. She never questioned anything that I said - she didn't cast any kind of judgment on things that I said. She listened. The questions that she asked were germane to what I was thinking, after I had expressed the thought. They were germane to my feelings about a situation. She has tremendous communication skills. And I think there are some people you meet

in life that you have an instant affinity to. She and I had that instant affinity."

Along with post traumatic stress disorder, panic attacks, and anxiety disorders, some survivors were being treated for chronic depression. Mary Ann had been in therapy "off and on" for about twenty years and said she was receiving the most help and support she had ever had in her life from her most recent therapist. She thought this was because her therapist's life experiences as a gay man had made him very non-judgmental of others,

> "I finally went to this really great doctor. I was really happy with him we got to be really good friends because, besides being my doctor, we were really good friends. I could tell him anything - he was just very non- judgmental, you know, and he would listen to me, and if I swore, it was not *'hush'* like … anyway I got a lot of support from him - kind of like - we used to call them, 'warm fuzzies' from him … I knew we were friends, before we said we were friends. It got to the point that, 'If I was okay to be his friend, then I must be okay' - you know."

Another survivor, Janice, said she had also received the most support in her life from a female therapist whom she had been seeing for about four years. She also thought that her anti-depressant medication was very helpful, along with regular attendance at her therapist's weekly women's group,

> "I have post traumatic stress disorder. It's like a reel in my head. It keeps turning and turning and turning. It's the same things. I think about the same things all the time. I replay the violent scenes, I do that, and the happy times with my kids. I try to remember those. I had two nervous breakdowns, so a lot of my memory is screwed up. I've got suicidal thoughts. I wonder, sometimes, what I would be like without my medication. It's a scary thought, because I wasn't taking any medication when I 'did myself' [slit her wrists], and my therapist … her patience, her knowledge, her understanding. She

truly cares about me. I really like her. I really like her a lot. It just seems like she gets to the heart, gets to the point - lets you draw your own conclusions and will guide you - kind of lead you in the right direction - very supportive. I get a lot from her. I'd be lost without her."

As these long term survivors explained, having the appropriate therapy and/or therapist can be beneficial. It can have a very positive effect on the life outcomes of victims and their children. Unfortunately, the need for skilled counselors, in particular for "talk therapists", is still **far** from being met, especially for those without adequate insurance or financial resources. The gravity and complexity of the mental and emotional problems that affect women and children after they leave should be better understood by survivors, lay persons, and families when they attempt to offer advice and help. For those who wish this understanding, an overview of some of major approaches to the treatment of domestic abuse victims are included in Chapters 10 and 11. Many of these have also been featured in popular self-help books and offer valuable tools and guidance toward further insight, self-discovery, and healing. These findings may also be of great interest to concerned family members and friends of victims. In some cases, even the batterer, himself or herself, may benefit from taking the time to understand more about the dynamics of abuse and victimization. The batterer, after all, may not only be the most recent perpetrator of violence, but also a prior victim.

CHAPTER SIX

SURVIVORS TALK ABOUT SUPPORT
AGENCIES • WORK • SCHOOL • CHURCH

The long term survivors I interviewed had turned to several other formal and informal sources of support for both short-term and long-term assistance. Social service agencies, workplace settings, schools, and church communities were all discussed and are evaluated by the survivors themselves in this Chapter. Some survivors also talked about the importance of personal spirituality as a means of healing from, and surviving domestic abuse.

Social Service Agencies

Battered women usually are very afraid after they leave the abuser and their fears have often been well-grounded, (Bowker 1983, 1986, 1993; Browne 1997; Ellis 1992; Geffner 1997; Gelles 1997). The ability to obtain employment, social service assistance, and/or welfare benefits can help provide needed material and instrumental support for survivors and their families (Dutton 1992; Kurz 1998; Raphael 2000). When employment opportunities are scarce, some survivors have trouble with the stigma associated with receiving welfare or food stamp assistance. They can also have trouble participating in welfare-to-work training programs (Browne, Salomon and Bassuk 1999; Murphy 1997; Raphael 1995, 1996, 1997, 2000). Non-participation in these programs, not only can hamper the survivor's ability to become more financially independent, she can also be penalized for noncompliance and prevented from receiving further welfare payments. This has caused increased concern among survivors, advocates, and experts, especially when the Cal Works and other state and federal "welfare-to-work" initiatives were more aggressively mobilized during the Clinton presidency (Ferraro 1996; Boyer 1999). Many of the survivors I spoke with, told me that they were impoverished, unemployed and rendered, at least temporarily, homeless after they left their abusers, so despite the stigma, welfare, food stamps, medical coverage or housing assistance were sought out by several women.

61

Only one woman said that she had received a feeling of support or compassion from anyone who worked at a social service agency. The majority of survivors found the monetary and material assistance very helpful, but said that agency representatives, themselves, were of little assistance (Chapter 6). This supports prior findings that social and welfare workers can sometimes exude a "blame the victim" mentality which can further objectify the victim, leading to more feelings of resentment and disempowerment on her part (Kurz 1998; Schillinger 1988; Eisikovits and Buchbinder 1996). Most survivors tended to perceive of welfare and case workers as intimidating, cold, or uncaring. In addition, the rules and regulations survivors often encountered when attempting to gain assistance could also be frustrating, confusing, or too restrictive. One survivor related the disappointment she had felt, when she finally began life on her own, and was forced to rely on welfare for the first time,

> "I'm on the County [welfare system] now. Never, never been on the County! I don't know what to do ... these people are being rude, crude, and abusive at the County office. Okay, I'm sitting here. I've just got away from somebody who has beat me black and blue, terrorized my children, and I've got to come to this and you're telling me this is the help you're going to give me?"

She added that the additional pressures resulting from the Cal-Works (welfare to work) programs, at the time, also made it very difficult for her to access the self-help, self-improvement, and healing that can be gained from attending battered women's groups, therapy sessions, or recovery group meetings,

> "... [A]nd now with this Cal Work thing. You don't know the neighborhood and you've got your children. The only way you can get around is on the bus. You've left the only home your abuser's provided - and sometimes those abusers provided very well. You've left all of that - to be in an apartment - probably a one bedroom with your four kids with the furnishings from the thrift store if you can find some ... and you're trying to function and

they're telling you, after you get home from work - after you get your kids together - to come to a meeting? Whose reality are they coming from? I didn't even have those kinds of pressures, and it took awhile before I could go out and seek help."

Interestingly, the two survivors who had worked for county agencies, themselves, in the past, found that their attempts to get short-term assistance were very successful. Despite this, they still did not consider welfare services a significant source of help. Their relative ease in gaining assistance might be attributed to already established connections with fellow workers, and/or to their own familiarity with related agency procedures, forms, and the benefits that were available.

The Workplace

Battered women tend to have higher general rates of unemployment, when compared to other groups (Strube and Barbour 1983). Even survivors who *are* gainfully employed, or are capable and willing to work, can still be negatively affected by long-term financial hardship after they exit (Kurz 1998; Davis and Kraham 1995; Lerman 1984). Starting out with limited funds, they are often less able to get secure employment, and, if they are employed, they can be negatively impacted by their vulnerability to being late, absent, or stalked by the abuser at or near their workplace (Zorza 1991). Despite these challenges, having the ability to engage in work or gainful employment remained a very high priority for most of the long term survivors with whom I spoke. Having a good job and a reliable income was seen as, not only materially helpful, but very empowering for survivors, as they began life on their own. Working regularly, or having a career, increased the survivors' positive self-appraisal, while providing her with a sense of independence. Interacting with others at the workplace was also valued highly by long term survivors, as a source of short term, and sometimes long-term, emotional, financial, and instrumental support.

Eight survivors said that interactions with others, during the time they spent at the workplace, were extremely helpful to them in combating isolation because it provided them with a sense of companionship and camaraderie with others. For some survivors, the close friendships they developed with fellow employees rivaled those formed in their families and neighborhoods. Cassandra found the workplace to be an empowering setting, because she was able to, not only *receive support from*, but also, to *provide support for*, fellow workers who were having problems, too. She described what she called the "levels" of spiritual growth her friends at work represented for her,

> "And I've noticed that, for me, there are different levels that I have gone through. When I was with the abuser, I was at one level, so I had one level of friends. It had to do with, not material, but a spiritual level. And when I got to this new office, the new group of friends were at a higher level - at the level that I was at the time ... yes, friends have been important."

Ellen said that her prior jobs in historically male dominated fields, such as construction, had created, what she called, her "basic support network". Before we talked, however, she had recently discovered great fulfillment through her second part-time job in a female dominated arena, as a crisis advocate for survivors of rape. In that position, she felt very empowered to render, what she considered was a very important service for rape victims that formal support systems are often unable to provide,

> "They all thank me, and they'll tell counselors that they work with afterward that I pulled them through - so I must be doing something right! That's all I wanted for myself and for the people I come into contact with - that I'm that anchor in that very terrible moment in their life, so that they have a source. The nurses - they collect forensic evidence - she's [the nurse is] not there to take care of the woman's emotional needs at all. And the police don't even know how to take care of their own emotional needs!"

For some long term survivors, getting a job again became a major turning point in their lives. Rachel, for instance, was already enjoying a supportive, non-abusive relationship with a new partner, shortly after she left her abuser, but being able to gaining employment again, seemed to play an equally large role in her healing. By enjoying the safety and security of her new relationship, she had at first become reliant on only her new partner for support. After their son was born, Rachel slowly became increasingly isolated from others, and as a result began using recreational drugs again "now and then". Eventually, one morning Rachel got out of bed and, in her own words, began to reclaim her life,

> "I'll never forget - it was on Easter morning. I got on a ten speed, I went over to Denny's, and I talked the manager into giving me a job. And that's when I stopped doing drugs. That's when I quit ... and I was taking awesome vitamins and I started saving money! I was really impressed with myself, too, that I was able to do that - it's amazing how much money you can save and have if you don't do drugs because I had so much more to show for it. I got a car and I saved five hundred bucks - to me that was a big deal, and my son was doing good. I'd enrolled him in a good school and was able to pay for the tuition. Yeah, for me that was good! And I loved going to work every morning. I loved it, I loved it!"

For Rachel, having a job again greatly increased her sense of independence and empowerment. She also gained self-esteem and evaluated herself more positively because she no longer had to rely on her new partner for support. By learning to take care of herself and being able to end her drug addiction Rachel's new sense of strength and autonomy was enhanced. As she developed more independence, her partner also seemed to respect her more. In turn, his positive appraisal of her efforts inspired Rachel to begin to approach her relationship with him as an equal, instead of as someone who was dependent on him and "weak".

In contrast, some of the other long term survivors I interviewed had eventually lost their ability to engage in gainful employment due to either or both physical or mental disabilities (some of them caused by earlier partner abuse). When this happened, their lives changed dramatically. The positive self-evaluation, connection to others and financial stability, they had formerly enjoyed in the workplace slowly disintegrated and disappeared. Mary Ann told me that working had provided her with substantial monetary and emotional support for many years, but eventually her back injury, combined with chronic major depression, had made her unable to keep working. She left her job as a graphic artist, the career she had been proud of for many years, which caused her self-esteem and social connection to plummet. All of a sudden, she found herself alone, with very little money, and without any form of support,

> "I went from an average of between five and seven hundred dollars a week to living on $250 a month with no job. Nobody helped me. I was on my own. I really wasn't getting any help anywhere. "

When she started feeling better, she renewed the relationship she had with her recovery group, got into therapy and went back to college. Mary Ann began to slowly gain additional support from teachers and friends, and then started assisting other disabled students. She soon began to really enjoy life again, along with her new improved self-image, and was later awarded the title "Disabled Student of the Year",

> "My whole life just changed totally. And it was working - everything I did was just like magic! It was really a trip. This was when he came into my life - one of my teachers. He was head of the Disabled Students program ... the first man I ever knew in my entire life who spent time with me and helped me and encouraged me without expecting a piece of ass in return. He was one of the finest men I knew in my life. He totally changed my life. He'd say things like, "My, you look lovely today," and at first ... it took me about six months to realize that he was doing that because he genuinely cared about me as a person, not as a piece of ass, or somebody he was going to get over on, but as a person ... that I was valuable to him and he respected me. And he had me counsel other recovering alcoholics, because it was something he

wasn't able to do, and he respected my ability to do it ... and then, later - I was helping disabled students, like myself, with memory loss, and my self-worth just soared and my self esteem just ... I became an entirely different human - somebody I liked. I mean when I was going to school it was like "Magic!" Everything turned out right."

Mary Ann's transformation demonstrates the positive outcomes that resulted from her new affiliation with *three* new major sources of support. First, her therapist provided her with emotional support. Then, members of her recovery group gave her additional support. Later, she began to receive even more support from her teachers and friends at college. Feeling affirmation from people that she trusted and respected, enabled Mary Ann to first empower herself - then, to do the same for others through her work with the disabled students she tutored. Throughout this process, she also learned new, improved ways of interacting in supportive environments, which further reinforced her new sense of self-worth.

School Settings

As Mary Ann has shown, college and educational settings can be meaningful, positive sources of social support for survivors. Returning to school has provided many prior victims of abuse with new and nurturing social interactions. School also offers hope. Seven survivors told me they had experienced a great deal of support in school settings at least one or more times in their lives. Four of them were still attending college, and one was going to adult school to get her GED. When victims had not been allowed by their abusers to pursue their education, going back to school after they got away, empowered them to experience meaningful support - outside of the negative, critical constraints of their marriage - which had been previously denied them. Going back to school meant meeting people who could provide them with affirmation, which positively affected the survivor's self evaluation and encouraged her to set additional goals. Going back to school meant, in essence, meeting those people who were willing to support a prior "victim's" new "survivor" identity.

Some disabled survivors found in educational settings an opportunity to formulate a new career plan for a job that would accommodate their disabilities. Unanticipated, but welcome relationships with men were also sometimes formed in college settings. For instance, Veronica met her new husband while attending community college. Although still facing many obstacles, she was determined to remain in school. She was in constant fear of being killed by her ex-husband, who continued to stalk and threaten her on campus for months after she left. Her fears escalated even further, when she learned that, only two years before, another young student and mother of three, had been murdered at a campus event by her estranged husband. Toward the end of Veronica's second semester back at school, she met a fellow student who would soon become the major source of support in her life. Robert slowly gained her friendship, provided her with a sense of protection, and then began to assist her financially. Robert and Veronica had been married for three years at the time I interviewed her, and were already the proud parents of two more children. She described her marriage as very happy, but sometimes difficult, because they were both still struggling to work full time, pay for child care, and to finish their college educations.

Church and Re*ligion*

I was surprised to discover that ministers, church groups, and formal religious settings were not considered strong sources of support by the majority of survivors with whom I spoke. Only four women told me that being a member of a church group, or attending church, had been an effective form of community or support for them. Although several women described themselves as "God fearing", "God loving" or "spiritual", they did not refer to themselves as religious. Most long term survivors did not participate regularly in organized religious groups or go to church. When a survivor had become alienated from religion, it had often been the result of feeling shame or judgment from others in the congregation, or in other church settings. It was interesting to note that, all but one, of the Caucasian survivors (Ellen), had shared this same experience of shame, feeling rejected, judged, or out of place in church settings. Ellen felt she had been blessed with a wealth of support from attending her present church. Formerly, as a member of her abusive husband's church congregation, she had always experienced religion to be very oppressive. Her recent affiliation with a Unitarian church, near her home, introduced her to other congregation members who were not judgmental or oppressive, but instead, very acceptant of her and of others. She was also pleased to see that female ministers played active, important roles in weekly church services,

> "I've kind of always had a spiritual side that had been untended - like a little garden full of weeds - and I found this congregation that I really like. You take responsibility for what you do, own what you've done. Own it - find out whether it's right or wrong. If it's not right for you, let it go and don't do it again - and don't carry the baggage with you. They accept everyone ...the ministers are predominately female and they're very open and very loving. It's very non judgmental - very loving. We sing 'Let there be peace on earth' in a big circle, holding hands, at the end of every service ..."

The three other survivors who found great comfort in church settings and considered their relationships with other church members to be important sources of support were African-American. All of these women told me they had a very close, intimate relationship with God, and professed their belief that faith, prayer, and regular church attendance would see them through any difficulty. Their shared perspectives may be due to the strong historical role of organized religion in the black community. Cassandra, who was African-American, said she had always been drawn to Church, as an enduring source of comfort, since she was a young girl. She was also very pleased, to tell me that, since she escaped her abuser, she was really enjoying her newly regained freedom again to engage more in religious practices, and had now become even more involved in church activities.

"As I've grown, I've always kind of fell back to that - remembering how I felt [at church] and mainly it was the music that attracted me. You know, like the beat, the words - everything was so nice about it! It always seemed ... it was like, you know, I wanted to go back to Church because I wanted to *hear that music!* That music always made me feel good and then, of course it brought me back ... then *that brought* me back to the Bible. Just before I met my ex, I was in the Bible and getting much more deeply into it ... what I should have done was kept my mind there instead of looking at him."

Dorothy who was African-American, said that being "in the church" and "knowing God and Jesus as her Savior", made her feel less alone in life and less afraid. She read her Bible everyday and had gained a new sense of peace and serenity from certain passages in scripture that she loved and had memorized. She shared some with me,

"You know, if I can keep focused on, and keep that embedded in my mind I can make it - like Psalm 27, 'the Lord is my hope and salvation - whom shall 1 fear?' ... 'The Lord is the hope of my life - of whom should I be afraid?' ... 'Even though my wicked enemies came upon me, to heed my flesh ... they stumbled and they fell!' Because - when you think about it, God is there. He never leaves us. He is always there with us. You know, sometimes, you may feel like, 'Damn, I have nobody. I'm all alone.' You're not. We have the Angels around us that watches us. And we have God himself."

CHAPTER SEVEN

SURVIVORS TALK ABOUT
FAMILY SUPPORT

Domestic violence destroys family life. The survivors I spoke with had all received various degrees of formal support and services, but they clearly indicated that either the availability or the absence of family or "family like" support played the most significant role in their long term survival. The importance of having this important form of assistance had come into play for many survivors, even before they met their abusers, then later after leaving them and for many years afterward. Material assistance from families was helpful, but more significantly, women talked, at great length, about the emotional component of family support throughout their lives. The perception survivors held of having, or of not having, family support, seemed to enhance, or conversely, to impede, their healing from abuse and feeling of normalcy. Ongoing interactions among family members also reinforced both former and current self-images that survivors held of themselves. Support from family also affected a survivor's coping and survival strategies and was related to her potential for being victimized again. Among the women I spoke with, five of the respondents credited the support of family as a very valuable part of ending the cycle of victimization in their lives and three survivors said that at least one family member had provided them with support.

Eight women said that they had *never* experienced any form of support from their families, although each of these survivors had the arguable benefit of having at least one living parent until adulthood. For these women, a lack of family support had strongly impacted their long-term life experiences in a negative way. The absence of family support among this group of women was also strongly correlated with childhood sexual, physical, and mental abuse, learning disabilities, alcoholism, addiction, and repeat victimization after they left their first abusers. (The various effects of support, or absence of support from family, friends, and pseudo family kinships, will be discussed later in this Chapter and in Chapter 8). Essential survivor needs, such as safety and protection will be explored, as well as self-evaluation and decision making - two important goal oriented behaviors that were deemed essential by survivors to be able to "stay out" long term.

Family Protection & Safety

Having support from a loving family helped survivors feel as if they were protected and safe. It provided them with the overall sense that they had a "safe haven" from the potential dangers of the outside world. Those who had a strong sense of family support were, typically, able to benefit from protective, loving parents and siblings, who showed deep concern for their welfare. Close networks of concerned, caring family members offered some of the women I talked to reliable help with the often unpredictable, exigencies of surviving on their own. These survivors expressed feeling all of their lives, that they were loved, cared for and supported, often by strong, nurturing mothers and/or committed fathers and, in particular, protective brothers. Devera, who came from a very large, strong, close-knit African American family, described the consistent reassurance and help she had received from them. Shortly after she returned to her abusive husband after four months of hospitalization for serious injuries his abuse had already caused, he began beating her with an extension cord. When they heard about this, her loving family came quickly to rescue her. Devera calmly describe to me the day her mother came to help her escape,

> "I'm like - Mom get me out of here! My Mom came ... and saw what she needed to see ... and we left. We finally got to the airport - my insides were shaking. ... I was in a wheelchair at the time. Mama had got us checked in by the time he closed the trunk of the car and he took off ... and I'm like, "Mom are we going to make it?" ... and she was like "We're making it baby" - and, I'm like praying ... holding myself the whole time - because he'd

> pulled me off planes before. Just shaking, praying. shaking, praying - and when the plane started backing up ... and when we hit the air and got off the ground ... [T]hat was the first day of the rest of my life."

Devera had also benefitted from the constant concern of her two brothers, who both quickly mobilized to secure her safety and protection. Both of them opened their homes to her until she could live independently. Not only did they provide shelter for her, they also helped her by regularly coaching her on ways to deal with the immobilizing fear she continued to experience during any interaction with her abuser,

> "That's where my brothers came in. They would answer the phone because I told them I don't want to talk to him, 'I'm not ready to talk to him', and they would get on the phone, 'Nope - you can't talk to her.' The first time I talked to him, I shook so hard on the phone. I'm sitting in a wheel chair with the phone to my face - and just *hearing* his voice terrorized me. So my brother took the phone ... and just hung it up! And he said, 'That's all you have to do is hang it up.' I said, 'Why can't I do that?' and he said 'You'll learn'.

In some cases, a survivor's family was unable to provide her with shelter after she left because doing so would jeopardize the entire family's safety. When this happened, supportive families would sometimes devise creative solutions for her immediate needs and protection. For instance, family members would collaborate with friends or coworkers, developing a sort of underground communication network. Through these clever arrangements, they were able to distract and divert the angry abuser from finding the survivor while at the same time, providing her with the material necessities she would need. Cassandra, after her month long stay at a shelter and a shorter "visit" with her brother in another state was empowered to regain the confidence and courage she needed to be able to return to her community, live with her parents and go back to her job,

"So the initial thing was ... I had places to stay. I had an

> uncle out of state who I was going to move with, and
> then I have family here, and my other brother had re-
> cently moved to Arizona. So, when I initially came out
> of the shelter, I went to visit my brother up in Oregon
> for about two weeks. So, I stayed out there for two
> weeks ... and then, after staying there, I was ready to
> come back here [to the family home]. So I came back
> here. I said to myself, "No, I'm going to stay here with
> my family. It's going to be safe here - it's going to be
> okay."

It was very interesting to discover after talking to survivors, that
the perception of having family protection and support was not,
necessarily, dependent on having an actual living family member
in their lives. June, a resilient, resourceful survivor who emphatically stated she had no *"real"* family support, told me that, instead, she relied on "visits" from two male family members whom
she had never actually even met. These *"men"* reliably provided
her with a feeling of safety and security, any time she was afraid.
"They" had just *"visited"* her a few evenings before we spoke, after she watched the film "You Can't Beat a Woman" during training at the domestic violence agency where she worked. Violent
scenes of a woman being beaten in the movie had brought back
memories of her own abuse and triggered symptoms of June's
PTSD. She told me these *"men"* always show up in her dreams to
protect her exactly at the times they are needed,

> "I believe that there's more than we see, I really do. I
> have a very strong connection with my dead twin. I be-
> lieve he is my protector and, when I was three or four
> years old, there used to be a man in a hat and a trench
> coat who would either stand in my bedroom doorway or
> sit on the foot of my bed until I went to sleep ... he never
> frightened me at all. I believe it was my father. The
> night we saw the video, it upset me so badly I couldn't
> sleep - all that night. I tried going to sleep in the bed -
> that didn't work. I went out to the den and tried to

sleep on the couch - that didn't work ... and I was still kind of shook up ... it really got to my core. About 5 o'clock in the morning I decided, "This is stupid. You've got to sleep in your own bed, and I got in bed and that man was standing next to the computer in my bedroom - and I haven't seen him since. Now it could be trick of the mind, you know ... I needed the protection of a protective figure in my life and I conjured him up. I don't care how he got there - but I slept that night peacefully because I felt protected."

Rachel also told me that feeling safe and protected after she escaped her abuser was not dependent on having actual biological family support. Instead, it was her perception, since childhood, that she was protected and cared for by a neighborhood man she always called "Dad". Rachel's "Dad" was actually the father of a girlfriend on her block who welcomed her into his home when she was eight years old, and had always provided an escape from the abuse of her adoptive mother. She still cherished the pile of letters her "Dad" had written to her after her abusive husband took her out of state. He kept begging her to return "back home" and it was he who finally helped her arrange her "getaway" over the telephone,

"Once we got there, I kind of felt stronger because I knew I had my Dad there. I just wanted to get away from him and call my Dad ... and my Dad said, "Go with him to his brother's house and I will be there". And, thank God, my Dad comes down the street in his car and gets out of the car and he looks at my ex - Bobby was petrified of my Dad - scared to death of him ... and I got in my Dad's car with my baby ... and I don't know what he said to Bobby, but he left right away ... and I left with my Dad and he told me I would be safe now which I was ... because he was scared to death of my Dad, which gave me a little bit of comfort because I knew he wouldn't mess with me. I thought, "I don't have to worry about shit with my Dad there." I wasn't scared - I would say

whatever I wanted with my Dad there, because I knew
he was there."

In the experiences Devera shared, we can see both the empowering material and emotional benefits gained through having a loving network of family support. In Ellen's interaction with her protective *"visitors"* during times of need in the form of her deceased brother and father, we are reminded that "feeling support" can also be created by the power of perception or what some might call the "spiritual" bonds of family. In Rachel's loving description of her devoted, protective "Dad", the parameters of family support were further expanded: *"family"*, according to Rachel, was what she and a biologically unrelated person created together and ultimately defined it to be. Her experience of close knit "pseudo family" or "fictive kin" support (see Chapter 8) came from the one person in her life who had always helped and truly cared about her, like a daughter.

Feeling Vulnerable

When long term survivors had no support from family of origin they tended to feel more vulnerable and unsafe. Feeling unsafe or unprotected was associated, among these women, with being more vulnerable to further abuse or to harm from others. All of the eight survivors who said they had never benefitted from family support had been abused, in some manner, by one or more family members, when they were children. Six of these women had also been sexually abused by a parent or other authority figure, as well. Multiple incidents of abuse from those close to them, had created, for these particular survivors, the perception they had never been safe or protected by anyone for an extended period. One survivor, victimized many times by family members, then by her husband and then, by future partners told me that survival had begun to mean to her simply managing to stay alive,

> "I'm still alive, with all the crap I've gone through. I've
> been shot at and I've had the shit beat out of me numerous times. I mean I can't even estimate how many

times, it's been so many times. Almost every guy I've gotten involved with has done it."

Those with no family support had to rely on only their own crea-tive resources, on friends, or on outside agencies for help and pro-tection when they left their partners. Ongoing attempts to gain safety often left them still uprooted, vulnerable, confused, and with contradictory feelings - hating that they had to rely on others for support, resenting they were ultimately forced to rely only on themselves - but at the same time, somewhat proud they always "made it on their own." Survivors who lacked family support and turned too quickly and to new partners for protection, tended to be victimized or abused again. Mary Ann, repeatedly sexually abused by family members as a child, expressed to me that, for her entire life, she had always felt as if she was in some kind of danger and when I initially asked when she first left her abuser, Mary Ann's reply was heart wrenching,

> "It's kind of hard to say because I was battered and abused and molested as a child and consequently, every relationship I've even been in, as an adult, has been abusive ..."

She went on to describe the patterns of patriarchal terrorism that had dominated her entire family and, therefore, the majority of her childhood and adolescent experiences,

> "My Dad was very violent. I used to get the crap beat out of me all the time - and my mother was very violent - the only kind of contact I had was from being smacked around. Even my mother ... at one time she was mad at me and she was ironing and turned around and hit me with an iron - and whatever she happened to have in her hand is what we got hit with whether it was a broom or the iron or, if she had a knife in her hand - we got the side of the knife."

Mary Ann also described to me in vivid detail, the sexual abuse she suffered, at the hands of her Uncle George, who forced her to have oral sex with him beginning when she was only three years old. Added to this was sexual molestation by her grandfather, and from another uncle who had fondled her since she was nine years old. During Mary Ann's childhood, there was no place in her home where she could feel safe. There was no one in her family to whom she could turn for protection. She had tried to report these incidents to her mother many times, but her mother, along with all of the other women in her family were too dependent on their husbands and brothers for financial support to really listen to her or to speak up,

> "This was my Uncle George who walked ten miles in the snow during the depression with cardboard in his shoes to support my mother and his wife and their five other siblings. No matter what anybody said he was ... like he was the patriarch of the family ... and no matter what he did - it was okay because he was Uncle George. They lived in Appalachia and in that area of the country, it's very common for people to molest members of their family. Incest is very common. I think it's because most of them are isolated. It's a couple of miles from home to home ... [A]and they lived in a tar paper shack - kind of like a lean to with wallpaper on it. All mother used to take to school to eat, if she was lucky, was a homemade biscuit with a little peanut butter on it, and if she wasn't so lucky, she would be able to take a cold boiled potato with no salt or pepper - just a cold boiled potato ... in my family you just don't talk about things like that [her sexual abuse]. If you don't talk about it, it "goes away" - and God forbid you should mention anything about Uncle George ... because he walked ten miles in the snow during the Depression, with cardboard in his shoes ... for a dollar a day!"

Sometimes a long term survivor had not been protected by family and then her lack of safety was compounded by the failure of outside agencies to intervene. When Dorothy, left her first abusive mate, the pimp who had beat and abused her from the time she was twelve years old, she could not turn to any of her family members for support. By that time, Dorothy had already learned that "the system" would not help her either. Abandoned by both of her parents at a young age, brutally abused in a foster home, and then neglected by the local child protective services, Dorothy, like Mary Ann, had never felt safe. She still had several scars all over her body from her early childhood, and later partner abuse. She related to me a long life history of one incident of abuse after another,

> "I don't know - I was so young when they came got me and took me from my Mom - I was like maybe six or seven. All I can remember was how I wound up in a foster home and had a problem wetting the bed ... so they would throw me down stairs into the basement. They would leave me with the dogs in the basement and feed me with the dogs. It was ugly - an ugly situation. I remember one morning I was going to school ... I was nine years old, and she had beat me real, real, bad - and I had big open welts on my back - real thick ones - and my fingers were busted open from trying to hold the belt to keep her from beating me ... [I] was laying my head down on the desk and I was sick behind the beating. So, when they took me to the nurses' station - I guess they were going to send somebody to the house, the foster people got scared and decided that the best way for them to get out of the problem was to get rid of me. So that's how I wound up on the bus when I was nine years old going to try and find my mother. They wrote an address on the paper that I gave to the bus driver."

Finding her mother, would not prevent Dorothy from enduring further humiliation, abuse and shame,

> "I was eleven and I was seeing a boy who was about 15 or 16, so I was sitting on the back porch, one day, and a lot of his buddies came and they all jumped me ... [A]nd they brought me downstairs, in the basement of the apartment building, and they started raping me, beating me, constantly beating me. They had me tied up and I

had to promise them that I'd do 'such and such' sexual favors before they would let me go. They let me out and I had no clothes on - nothing - and I finally ran up into my apartment ... [A]nd I really can't say to this day if my Mom heard me screaming or hollering - because I was screaming and screaming - and my eyes were all swollen up because they was constantly beating me. So when I got to the house my mom was yelling at me and she said, "Get yourself up, you tramp - you slut - you trumpet! Get in the tub and take a bath" and it was crazy. So, I don't know if she knew what was going on and she was afraid of the gangs, or what - but nothing more was ever said about that. And then, she sent me away - again - to live with my aunt."

A year later, Dorothy had run away from her aunt's home and began living with an older man, who would soon become her first abusive partner. He beat and exploited her for two years, perpetuating a cycle of abuse that led to two more marriages that were abusive. According to Dorothy, this twenty four year cycle of perpetual abuse led to her misuse of alcohol and drugs, her frequent changes of residence, and to several episodes of homelessness. In fact, Dorothy was homeless at the time I interviewed her.

Another long term survivor, Laurie was also homeless for the ninth time, feeling unsafe, staying in a shelter, along with three of her four children at the time I interviewed her. Her repeated domestic abuse incidents had caused complaints from neighbors, and, ultimately, her eviction from rental housing again. Laurie also described her mother as the first in a long line of abusers. Her first husband beat her repeatedly, so she left him, and soon married another man "for protection". She became pregnant with their first child and her new husband began beating her. After escaping again, she turned to a third mate, "for protection", who became even more violent than the others had been. For the fourteen years, prior to when we talked, Laurie had been beaten by every man she had ever known, and had come to believe that danger followed her everywhere she went. Even while she was talking with me, she was constantly looking behind her, as if expecting a blow from someone. It appeared to me that, perhaps, Laurie was suffering from untreated post traumatic stress disorder and when I mentioned this, she told me that she had not been able to receive treatment from mental health services, because she was not considered "sick enough", due to state mental health cutbacks. Laurie admitted she was really stressed out and afraid, but said that she finally had thought of a solution. As soon as she left the shelter, she was going to start hanging out with bikers and skin heads, so that maybe their presence near her would make everyone *"just leave her alone"* and then, she could finally feel safe. I noticed that she had recently shaven her head nearly bald,

> "Short hair pisses them off because they can't pull you around by your hair anymore. My motto is 'It's a man's world' They conquer the world. The women civilize it - and women should be angry too, because we're taking too much shit."

Nearly six months after Laurie's interview, I received an urgent voicemail message from her. She sounded extremely distressed. Unfortunately, I was unable to reach her when I attempted to return her call. I have often wondered how her "skinhead" solution worked out. Did she finally find protection or more violence in her life? What the experiences of Laurie, Mary Ann, and Dorothy have shown us is the long-term negative effects that can result from lack of family support, especially when that is coupled, with multiple incidents of early family abuse. In contrast, it is easy for us to recognize the protective benefits, of having a truly supportive family, when this is juxtaposed against the physical and emotional endangerment experienced by lifelong victims of family abuse and mistreatment.

Family Support: Self Evaluation

As stated in Chapter 4, gaining and maintaining an improved evaluation of self is an important factor in being able to "stay out", recover from abuse, and end former patterns of victimization. When survivors had supportive families, leaving the abuser mobilized not only a physical reunion with family members, but also a return to the self-affirming family *values and perspectives* that they were already familiar and comfortable with. Raised in non-violent, nurturing homes, the negative perceptions about themselves they fell victim to, when living with their abusers, were an extreme departure from what they had experienced during earlier interactions within their family of origin. Cassandra, for instance, was quick to describe a clearly, heightened image of herself, one shared by other survivors who, also, had close family support,

"I wasn't raised to be this way - an abused woman."

Survivors who did not have support from family tended to have less positive expectations for themselves and tended to evaluate themselves more negatively. This inferior view of themselves had already taken root during childhood; it was not simply a result of their adult relationship with an abusive mate. Survivors with no family support expressed the perception that the verbal and physical abuse they had experienced with him was no significant departure from earlier expectations about what family life should be like. Marital and domestic abuse, was, in the words of, at least, two survivors I spoke with, "just the same old thing - the same old thing, all over again." As we have seen, physical, mental, emotional, and in some cases, sexual abuse, had been a part of what these women had expected as common family experience since they were little children.

Reunion with Family As Value Reinforcement

For women with family support, their physical reunion with family members, after they left abusers, seemed to represent a "symbolic" reunion with familiar family values and shared perspectives. Being with their families again, enabled them to quickly notice the deep contradiction between the nurturance and values they shared at home, and the destructive interactions they had experienced during life with their abusers. With their families' loving assistance, these long term survivors were able to utilize "reunion" with family as a springboard from which to reclaim earlier positive self-images, first created and enjoyed within their close family networks. These survivors tended to think of themselves as being intelligent, capable, being able to learn easily, and goal-oriented. They also expressed stable, positive assumptions about the world generated very early through family interactions. Devera spoke about her supportive family often and about the feelings of nurturance and self-esteem she had experienced as a child. With her family's support, those early feelings began to return almost immediately, after she left her husband, and reunited with them,

> "My parents always supported everything I did. When there were recitals or performances I would do, they were there - half the neighborhood was there ... [A]nd my father had a way about him that embraced the world - our world - my world - and when I explain this to my friends, they say, "Wow - you really did grow up in a fairy tale", but that's how my parents wanted us to be brought up - in a safe environment. We had that freedom to be children. Our parents didn't force us to be adults before our time ... and Grandma took care of me when I was a baby while mom and dad worked. I could always call my grandmother, no matter what. I was spoiled by the family as a whole. My parents were very protective. I was protected. I had two brothers that protected me, so, when this situation with my husband happened ... that's why we broke up the first time, because I wasn't going to put up with his stuff. If I had stuck to my guns, in the first place - I would have been all right, but I wavered in that resolve - and that's where I messed up."

Cassandra also credited her father's example, along with her upbringing as the middle child in a large loving family, for instilling in her the competitive edge she would need to pursue her goals. She referred to the "go getter" personality that motivated her immediately to regain a sense of independence and self sufficiency, after she left her husband. When we talked, she was in the process of pursuing her original goals again, as well as creating new ones,

> "My father - when we were going to school, he would work two jobs, if he had to, to support us in whatever we needed to do. And one summer I did the same thing - I held two jobs, two full-time jobs at one time, but I was like, "This is something I need to do", and for me it was normal. "My dad did it so must be okay" ... "Anybody can do it", so I did it! And as a middle child you kind of learn to rely on yourself - it's like you've got that competition against the person older than you, so you're always going to try to do better. Once you start that in yourself, then it continues - you can't stop it. Like the "It's okay" - kind of "settled" type of thing ... I've never settled - it's like knowing your dreams. My family never raised me to be this way ... an abused person."

Rachel, who described the surrogate father she referred to as "Dad" earlier had struggled with abandonment and self-image issues, for many years, because she had been "given away" when her own mother didn't want her, and then, was later disliked and abused by her adoptive mother. Again, she was very quick to emphasize several times, the supportive role her surrogate "Dad" had played in helping her build, her self esteem and confidence, and then later, to rebuild it again. "He was always there" and "always on my side", she said, reassuring and encouraging her during her childhood and after she left her violent husband,

> "It was my Dad, my Dad, he knew how to comfort - and he kept making me think, to realize that I didn't have to settle for second best - that I was beautiful, and that, you know - that I could do so much better. It took a long time for all that to sink in, you know, because he had told me over and over again, you know, "You're so pretty. You can get anyone you want." He had told me so many times that I was smart, too, and could do so much better - that I could do so much better, and I didn't believe him ... and it took a long time to believe him, but, I

finally thought, "You know, you're right. You're right -
I really can do better" and I have ... I have."

Rachel, Cassandra, and Devera have all described, in their own
words, the influential role that family or "family like" support
played in their overall evaluation of themselves. Being consistent-
ly cared for, protected and highly valued, enabled them to perceive
the partner abuse they had experienced as a deep contradiction
from earlier images they held of themselves. Reuniting with family members who loved, affirmed and supported them also facili-
tated their newly found "survivor" identity – evaluating themselves again as capable, attractive, intelligent, valuable women,
worthy of having a loving home.

Lack Of Family Support
Self-Evaluation

Survivors with no family support did not perceive their relationship with the abuser, to be a departure from their early family
experiences. Instead, the relationship with their husband or
partner was often referred to as a mirror or repeat of earlier negative childhood interactions with family members or significant
others. Verbal and physical abuse by new partners also further
reinforced the survivors' feelings of powerlessness and childhood
entrapment. As one woman stated "... the same thing - and I still
had no place to go."

Some women said they had always felt like outsiders within their
own families, "always feeling" as if they were "black sheep",
"bad", "different", "crazy" or "mixed up". It had taken Mary Ann
a series of relationships with many abusive men, along with
nearly twenty years of therapy, several college psychology classes,
and her committed involvement in recovery groups, to recognize
the effect that family abuse and lack of support had wreaked on
her self-image. By the time we talked, she had come to realize
that her childhood mistreatment had made her more prone to
multiple abusive partner relationships. She had also started to

take note of a similar pattern of behavior in others - in particular, in violent men,

> "Now I understand it. It's because I thought I didn't deserve any better, and the only kind of man that was attracted to me was violent men because I was a bad person and that's all I deserved. I think it happens on a metaphysical level, I do - because it's kind of, like another alcoholic knows another alcoholic. You sense it - it's kind of like [an] "it takes one to know one kind of thing". And just about everyone I have met in AA has been a victim of some kind of abuse - almost 100%, you know, and most of the time, it's not just physical abuse - it's some form of molested. The ones that hit me the hardest were the Bikers sitting there - these big bad Bikers sitting there with tears in their eyes – talking about their father having sex with them or their uncle or their neighbor 'doing them …'"

Yvonne had also always felt like an outsider, isolated, even in her own large Latino family. She expressed the pain she felt as a child, when she was told, repeatedly, how stupid and bad she was. She suspected that this had created a very negative effect on how she, later, saw herself as an adult,

> "I think more different from my mom and my family and them. There's nine of us but were not close. There's like maybe one or two out of the nine that I could maybe talk to. I was the black sheep. I really was because they always titled me that way. It's hard to get out of it - meaning mentally, when you're so deep mentally in there you can't find a way out. It's hard. Your mind just goes on and on and on and on and on and - since you're so drilled in there that you're stupid … 'You're stupid. You're stupid. You're stupid. You're an idiot. You're ugly. You're no good. You're stupid. No one wants you. You're this. You're that.' It just stays with you. It fuckin' scars you up forever. There's times that I feel like that too - because of the writing problem-

and because of all that drilling by my husbands too -
them calling me 'pee-wee brain' for 10 plus years of all
my life. And even when I was a child my Mom used to
abuse me, 'Oh, you're so stupid. Oh you're so stupid' …
all the time hearing this negative shit. How do you expect to get ahead in life, if you're always hearing the
negative from birth to adult?"

Yvonne and other long term survivors who had no family support
also described themselves as "being stupid". Six women among
those with no family support, still suffered from learning disabilities which they thought had negatively impacted their financial
well-being and life opportunities. It may be of interest that six of
the seven women with learning disabilities had also been sexually
molested as children by a family member or other authority figure. Yvonne admitted that she had been struggling since she left
her second abusive husband for several years, with the help of a
disabled student's tutor, to finish her Bachelor Degree. At the
time we spoke, she only needed three more classes to attain her
goal, but two of these were math and she feared she would be unable to complete them. There was also a required writing compe-
tency test which, as an ESL student with dyslexia, Yvonne was
almost certain she would fail. Deeply in debt from student loans,
and barely able to pay her monthly living expenses, she expressed
deep frustration with herself and at times, grave pessimism about
her future,

> "I'm below poverty. I'm really not proud of anything be-
> cause I'm still in the same hole. I feel I haven't accom-
> plished anything really. If one of my dreams would
> come true - which none of them do … like getting a good
> career - that would make me feel like I did finally ac-
> complish something that I want to accomplish. And I'm
> not accomplishing it. I'm not even near it and realisti-
> cally, I can't do it because it involves writing or math or
> it involves some kind of stuff that I don't know so I can't
> do it. So I hate part of me because I'm so stupid. It
> pisses me off! That's bullshit. People have got these
> good jobs [in the criminal justice system]. They're

smart, but they don't even belong in that job and I'm not smart, but I belong in that damn job … you know - because I can relate to these youth or to these people who have problems, but I don't get the damn job. I'm lacking something. The problem is I don't know how to spell and when I know there's spelling involved I just freak out. I just freak and I know I can't do it and it really upsets me and I say, 'What do I have to be so fucking stupid for?'"

Janice, who was repeatedly beaten and sexually victimized by her father, brother and first husband also said that she always had trouble with mathematics, especially her timetables and her adult daughter was having trouble with math too. Although she had never been formerly diagnosed with learning disabilities, Janice was "certain" her IQ was not high and laughed as she said,

"All my life, everybody's told me I was stupid. My father, my mother when I was growing up brothers and sisters, both husbands. Jimmy has told me I'm stupid - not smart enough. Anything I did. If you didn't do something right, you were stupid, 'What's the matter - you stupid or what? That kind of stuff. My older brother, the one who molested me when I was little - my Dad used to tell him he was stupid almost every day, and my brother grew up feeling stupid and had a really hard time in school. In the back of my head I'm thinking, 'Well good.'"

Long term survivors Janice, Mary Ann and Yvonne clearly explained in their own words, the destructive long-term effects that lack of support and victimization within their early family environments, rendered upon their ongoing tendency to evaluate themselves negatively. Family members or other authority figures abandoned them or abused them, and, sometimes, even blamed them for the abuse that they endured. As we have seen, earlier sexual abuse among these women was also associated with learning disabilities, repeat victimization and long-term drug or substance abuse.

Family Support: Problem Solving

Supportive families provided long term survivors with help in decision-making and problem-solving after they fled their abusive partners. The importance of effective problem-solving was discussed earlier in Chapter 4. When women came from large connected families, they were frequently able to solve financial problems more effectively, through increased material resources, and instrumental assistance from family members. Strong family support also seemed to increase the survivor's confidence that she was able to problem solve and possessed the strength to survive, independently. One survivor, Michelle, age 39, said that her early upbringing, along with loving family support, made the decision to leave her abuser, after the first time he hit her very easy. She said that her father had raised her to be a tomboy, to know how to fight back, remain strong and to value her independence,

> "I was used to doing for myself. I learned how to fight a long time ago. I've had some bruises along the way, but I'm not going to take it. No way. I left him the first day he did it [hit her] and I took everything - that was it!"

"The Family Meeting"

Families who provided effective problem-solving assistance were quick to bring together their collective resources and work closely together. Family members would sometimes work covertly, behind the scenes. Devera, who described her very supportive family earlier, told me that family members from all over the United States, gathered at her brother's home the day after she left her abuser. They held an informal meeting to collectively assist in determining the best personal survival strategies to undertake during the months ahead. During that meeting, many members in her family gently coached and guided her toward deciding the best solutions for her. Then, they continued to meet with her and problem-solve, until she felt more secure and confident in making her own decisions by herself. Devera described the process in detail for me,

"It was sort of like a family meeting. All the family was there. My daughter, both my brothers, and my Mom were there and that was basically what we were there for was to figure out, 'Okay, now what?' Because, like I said before, I have my family to back me up, unlike a lot of women who have no one. So, that was the first question that was posed to me by my older brother, 'Okay, what do you want to do. What's the plan?' And I'm like, 'I just got here. I don't know.' And, I didn't. I didn't have a clue. So it was, 'Okay, you can have today to think about it. What do you want to do and how do you want to do it?' I had to go sit outside on the hillside behind his house. Very peaceful. And when you're in turmoil, things like that *are* ... [T]he next day I had to have a plan. So, I would think a little - very helpful to get your thought processes going - and go ask them questions like, 'Are you willing for me to stay with you?' All of them said 'Yes', so then I had to think about, 'Which one did I want to live with?'"

Devera went on to describe the process that *she* went through, herself, as she began to consider the various options that her family had made available to her. They provided her with, just enough time, to weigh the benefits, along with the potential drawbacks, of each family member's offer of assistance. She carefully deliberated, using her intimate familiarity with most of the members of her family, to predict who could provide the best particular type of support she needed to heal, rebuild and improve upon her life,

"My mom lived in a rural area and, at that time, because of my injuries, I had to be going to the doctors at least four days a week. There was so much damage to my organs to repair and more surgeries. My brother, Mike - he's a thinker-planner person, and he would have provided me with whatever was necessary for me to get well, and I knew that, but he would have empowered me with the ability to sulk - sit and sulk, simply because he would leave it up to me to develop my plan and make it happen. Whereas with my younger brother, Eric, he's' the tough love strategy, "The plan is there - do it!" And there's a subtle difference, but I recognize the difference - because I knew Eric would make me *do*. Action is definitely his emphasis. So, I worked with the family on "The Plan". Number one was to get well. Number two was to go back to school."

Because Devera was very closely connected to her family and familiar with the personalities and lifestyle characteristics of each member, she was able to make a well thought-out, informed decision about which of her loved ones would be able to offer the most effective forms of support. Her family's ability to offer assistance without pressure, blame, judgment, or conflict, allowed her the freedom to make the decisions that she, herself, thought would benefit her the most, over the long term. Devera's family also continued to offer financial and practical assistance and offered feedback and advice to her, until she became more comfortable with her own independent, problem-solving, and decision-making ability again. According to some domestic violence experts, the efforts taken by Devera's devoted family, would encapsulate the combination of connection and autonomy that represent ideal support (Stark and Flitcraft, 1998).

Lack Of Family Support: Decision Making

The long term survivors I spoke with that had no support from their own families, usually had only themselves to rely on during important decision-making junctures in their lives. Having very limited or more often, a complete lack of financial assistance from their families, they were also usually more limited in other resources when they left their partners. As a result, very important decisions were often predicated by their immediate survival needs or even sometimes just by impulse due to overwhelming emotions such as anger, fear, or loneliness. Sometimes they would solicit advice from friends, but more often, as stated earlier, they would turn to a new partners for problem-solving and direction. This typically, set the stage for future domination, when the new partner became controlling, and mentally and/or physically abusive. Domination and abuse by another new partner, then, further impeded the survivor's ability to make their own, independent choices, thus limiting their freedom and perpetuating a sense of helplessness and shame.

Most survivors, with no family support had regretted later, the impulsive decisions they had made. They perceived many of their prior choices as *"the same mistakes over and over again."* Feelings of frustration and shame sometimes led to the short or long-term overuse of food, alcohol, street, or prescription drugs. For example, Dorothy had started using alcohol by the time she was twelve years old, in her attempt to numb herself from the shame she felt after her gang-rape. After three abusive husbands, who had all embarrassed and ashamed her in front of friends, she became progressively more socially isolated and alienated. She began to feel "stupid" and lost confidence in her ability to *"say the right thing"* or to make everyday decisions. Finally, Dorothy decided to avoid all social contact in order to avoid the shame of making more *"stupid mistakes"*. After months of isolation, she sunk into a deep depression,

> "I kept a lot of stuff inside. I would just keep it to myself - and I started letting myself go. I started gaining weight and I stopped working ... I just sat up under the TV - never went anywhere. I never even went out with the kids, whereas I used to take them to Disneyland Magic Mountain - all these different places, I just stopped. I became like a "Functioning Vegetable", because I was there, but I wasn't. I was coherent, but I was incoherent, you know. I don't know - I felt like I was bad news to people because, every time I got with my friends before, I was always in a relationship and there was always some kind of abuse or fights. So I just felt like, "God - maybe ..." I was thinking that that was how they was thinking", Oh here she comes and her abusive boyfriends or her abusive husband. There's gonna' be a fight." So, I felt better if I just stayed away."

Like Dorothy, other survivors, with no familial support were usually quick to blame themselves for "all the wrong decisions" they
had made. Their families often blamed them, too. When Yvonne
left one abusive husband, and later another, her family did not
support her decision to leave either time. Instead, they strongly
adhered to the traditional idea of remaining married, despite the
repeated incidents of domestic abuse she had suffered. Feeling
ashamed and isolated, Yvonne went through a long time period
when she was addicted to the prescription tranquilizer Valium,
just so that she could, in her words say 'The Hell with it!'"

> "I don't know. I always chose the wrong people. I don't
> know why but it sucks. My Mom would say negative
> stupid shit like 'Oh well, go back with Jose' or they
> would say it was my fault or shit like that. Why is it my
> fault? Why me? Oh yeah, they're always thinking it was
> my fault - my fault! And I go 'Why - why was it my fuck-
> ing fault?' 'Oh, John's a good man.' 'What happened
> with John?' and 'He's such a good guy.' Like it's my
> fault all the time! They would always put blame on me.
> I started using Valiums. I was addicted to my Valiums.
> I used to get them in the 50 or 100 bottle and I used to
> get the 10 milligram - I used to be hooked on those suck-
> ers, tremendously hooked on my Valiums. I used to mix
> them with alcohol all the time, but I just wanted to block
> out everything, so I would mix it. I used to get really
> loaded on it …so I used to be a really bad girl …"

Mary Ann also further described how she believed her childhood
abuse, along with her mother and stepfather's distorted idea of
"protecting" her had influenced her poor choices of men,

> "I went from a battered and sexually molested relation-
> ship at home to battered sexually abused relationships
> with men. I was having severe financial problems, but I
> would always get involved with these guys who, instead
> of them supporting me, I ended up supporting them. I
> told one guy to get out, and he got real violent and we
> broke up - and then, I started dating another guy who

> drug me out of the bar where I worked and tried to kill
> me. [I]t was like I was a magnet for violence - every-
> where I went - I was attracting all these darn violent
> men ... no matter where I went."

In their own words, some of the long term survivors in this group, "just couldn't seem to avoid picking abusive men". Lacking safe, affirming and predictable interactions with significant others, during their early lives, the unpredictable nature and potential danger of interacting with others was familiar to them. Unpredictable or negative interactions in their adult lives further reinforced their sense of poor decision-making abilities, self-blame and shame. These negative feelings sometimes led them to adopt destructive coping strategies, such as overeating, drug or alcohol use in their failed attempts to numb the shame they experienced, due to, what they perceived of to be, "their own mistakes.'

Long term survivors attempted to obtain social support from various formal and informal sources, again and again, as you have seen in recent Chapters. A domestic violence shelter was used by only one survivor who said she found her stay there very helpful. Police, courts, legal services, and social service agencies were generally ineffective forms of support, according to many survivors. Representatives of these systems often made survivors feel angry, frustrated, or ashamed. Church groups, recovery groups, and mental health services received mixed ratings as potential sources of support. In contrast, workplace and school settings were evaluated as very important sources of support, for many of the survivors I spoke with, providing needed financial resources, along with opportunities to rebuild a positive self-image. Support from family of origin, when it was available, was also rated as very helpful to nearly half of the women with whom I talked. Family support provided safety, help with decision making, material assistance, help with children, and a positive sense of self.

When family support was limited or unavailable, survivors tended to experience more difficulties. Lack of family support was correlated with ongoing conflict, or some form of abuse, among family members. For six survivors, absence of family support was coupled with both sexual and physical abuse within family of origin. Patterns of repeat victimization, after leaving their abusers, was more common for these survivors, as were learning disabilities and a propensity for legal, illegal drug abuse. These behavior patterns, and coping mechanisms, seemed to make overcoming domestic abuse more difficult for survivors in this group. Frequently, it also led to self blame. Lack of family support was also associated with negative self evaluation, lack of material and childcare assistance, impulsive decision making, shame, isolation and the use of other self-destructive coping mechanisms.

It was also interesting to note that most of the survivors I spoke with who had no family support, also tended to have difficulties gaining assistance from other informal, and even formal sources of social support. Gaining and maintaining new connections with others, after they left their abusers, was also extremely difficult for many of the long term survivors who had no support from family of origin. It was even more difficult, if they were poor, lacked adequate transportation, and/or other social resources in the community. This was especially true, when the survivor suffered from long-term physical disabilities, chronic pain, and/or post traumatic stress disorder. Isolation and lack of connection with others also caused survivors who did not have a close network of support, to be more prone to loneliness, depression, social alienation and to repeat victimization.

"When you need to be loved, you take love wherever
you can find it. When you are desperate to be loved, feel
love, know love, you seek out what you think love should look
like. When you find love, or what you think love is, you will lie,
kill, and steal to keep it.   But learning about real love comes from
within.   It cannot be given. It cannot be taken away.   It grows
from your ability to recreate, within yourself, the essence of loving
experiences you have had in your life."

Iyanla Vanzant

CHAPTER EIGHT

SURVIVORS TALK ABOUT
RECREATING & RECONSTRUCTING FAMILY

FICTIVE KIN• PLAY FAMILY • NEW RELATIONSHIPS

Survivors with family support seemed to readily expand their available support system to include "family like" relationships with others, both at the workplace and in the wider community. These additional relationships provided women with a sense of connection and sometimes extended the survivor's material and social resources over the long term. Cassandra, who lauded the value of her own family and her workplace as support systems, went on to describe the very close relationship that she enjoyed with one particular woman at her workplace,

> "I moved to a new office and then I met a new group of friends - and they were always very supportive and when we were in the prayer group they would pray for me and for my baby ... and [when the baby was born] my one friend - I called her the morning I went to the hospital ... and she was there when I had my son. So she always says that she's the "other mother" of my son ... [A]nd now my son's godmother and I became the closest of friends to a point where at the time she was going through things where she didn't want friends, because she had been hurt by friends - the more she tried to push me away, the more I told her, "I don't care what you're used to about pushing people away, but you're not going to push me away like that because I'm going to be around" so yeah - I have a lot of friends and they seem to keep growing."

Other survivors, with only limited support from their own biological family members, were able to expand and access social support through what they called "family like" or "play family" relationships with friends, coworkers, and counselors or mental health providers. Betty and her children were still in therapy due to her ex-husband's prior abuse, at the time we spoke. She told me that, although she had benefited from the support of two siblings, she still placed significant value on relationships, developed over the years, with two female therapists, especially her children's' therapist, whom she described as "like a family member",

> "The therapist that I have now - she's not actually my therapist - she's my kids' therapist. She is like an extended family member. She comes over - anything that goes on - whether it's with me, or with my kids. She's just like a phone call away. I pick it up and she's there to listen, no matter what it is. And my sisters are helpful. Me and Nicole - we call each other every morning."

In contrast, survivors who had never benefited from the support of their own families told me that maintaining close, supportive connections with others, in the outside world, had been much more difficult, over time. When Dorothy left her first abuser, she had only the support of her "play family" - close friends and neighbors in her, largely African-American, community. "Play family" are closely connected pseudo-family or surrogate family groups, also referred to in academic literature, as "fictive kin" (Stack 1974) Whenever she was beaten, when her children were young, her "play family" provided her with sympathy and moral support; they also helped Dorothy in many other ways, such as giving her assistance with child-care and child-rearing,

> "I had moved in with this woman and we were really close, so I would call her my Aunt - because she was like an Aunt to me. And she had kids, so they were like my sisters. I just felt like - like they took over and accepted me in their family - and so, after I had my daughter, I moved with her so she could help me raise my two children. Like right now, today - we're still close. I still go to their family reunions, and when I go down that way, I always make it a point to visit her. And when I had my daughter they just spoiled her rotten - somebody was

always holding her or always had her - so I called her 'their baby.'"

Ellen, who had also never experienced any support from her own family of origin, did manage to gain "family like" support, through her long-standing relationships with two "play sisters." She had developed close friendships, with these two women, at two different work settings during her recent past. Ellen and her two "play sisters" were all looking forward, at the time we spoke, to the day when they buy a big house, in the South, where they planned to spend their retirement years, living together. She said that she had also gained "family-like" connections with others by "parenting" those who had been affected by violence. As a rape crisis advocate, she was, in her own words, an "Earth Mother," nurturing and protecting rape victims, during what she thought was their greatest moment of need,

> "They've got to have an anchor - the "Mother Earth" figure. Nine times out of ten, I'll walk in and I'll be just making an open arm gesture ... and nine times out of ten, they want to be held. That's the first thing they want - they want to be held. They want to be able to cry on your shoulder and just get past that - and just go on. I've only had one [rape victim] who didn't want to be touched. She couldn't make eye contact. She had been raped from the time she was two until she was eleven years old by a family member and she was just, "Do this. Get it over with. I want to go home."

Unfortunately, Dorothy and Ellen's semblance of "family-like" support and close, nurturing connection were not common among the other long term survivors who had not experienced support from their own birth families. More often, after repeated incidents of abuse and victimization, this particular group of women was prone to becoming even more withdrawn, and isolated from other others. Some of these survivors said that they began to self-medicate with legal or illegal drugs and/or alcohol for long periods. However, these women were sometimes able to, later, gain the benefits of "family like" or "pseudo family" support, through their intermittent, or long-term, involvement in alcohol or addiction recovery groups. For Mary Ann, being at an A.A. meeting truly felt, to her, as if she finally had found a place where she could be cared about, and listened to - where she could feel "at home".

New Partners

Six long term survivors described their new partners as the major source of support in their lives. Having a non-abusive mate, provided them with the perception that they finally had a "normal life (see Chapter Five: Goal 5), one characterized by a new sense of balance and predictability. Their successful relationships with new men provided them with increased material and monetary support, as well as the restoration of highly-valued nuclear family units. This enhanced the survivor's sense of social respectability, along with her self-image, as a successful, loving, wife and mother. Some women said they were relieved to have found a man who would allow them freedom, but who was, at the same time, still deeply devoted to them. In some cases, they were grateful their new partner provided a good "father figure" for their children. One survivor, Christine, met her new partner less than a year after her abusive relationship ended. Her abuser had spent all of her $60,000 inheritance, and then, gone to jail, leaving her with only one valued material possession in life – her computer; this was interesting, since a few months later, she would meet her new partner, on her computer, in an internet chat room. She had carefully checked out the character profile provided for each chat room participant, and then, finally, selected her new partner to chat with, because he worked for the defense department. The fact that he had a security clearance made her feel more comfortable and safe about meeting him,

> "He couldn't be totally wacky with a security clearance," she told me, as she smiled warmly, and laughed for a moment.

After they got to know each other, Lloyd admitted to her that he had also been abused, both mentally and physically, by his ex-wife. Christine and Lloyd began dating, and by the time I interviewed her, they had already been married for three years. She said that she was extremely happy and, for once in her life, she finally felt secure,

> "He's a terrific guy. I couldn't ask for anything better. He's a perfect person - a really great person. I don't work. He totally supports me and he gave me his truck. My daughter's back with me and she worships her little sister. I couldn't ask for a better situation - I feel 100% totally secure."

Christine's experience was rare. Most of the long term survivors took far more time to become totally committed to a new relationship, even if the man they were involved with was not abusive. It was only after Betty had lived with her new partner for over twelve years that she finally trusted him enough to marry him. She said that she had received a great deal of support from him, and that she found great fulfillment in the large blended family they had created together. This included her own children, the children they had together, foster children, an adopted child, and an eagerly awaited new baby.

> "You know I can actually say I am happy. I've got my own kids. I've got the baby coming. I've got Jeremy and I've got Billy - and now, I have Isaac, so I'll soon have eight kids. Those kids are my life, and with my ex there wouldn't be no Jeremy, no Billy, and no Isaac. He doesn't believe in taking anyone in - helping anybody do anything. And my oldest son's life is a lot better now! He and my husband have been buddies forever. They just get along. [T]he only time I ever have a remembrance of my ex is like violent TV shows, or stupid things like that - and when I actually have to confront him or see him or talk to him about the girls or anything like that. But, other than that - No. I'm happy where I'm at now, and doing what I'm doing now, and you know what I'm saying … my new life,

Betty said that her new marriage was not "perfect," but she was still glad to be able to do what she, and other survivors referred to as "normal things," and to have someone "normal" for a husband,

> "Now George is no piece of cake, either, but it is nothing near - near ... I mean ... he is 85% reliable, plus he is good with my kids. That's the difference. He likes to do things together with the kids and this and that. He enjoys my family. My friends can come over - he's more involved and I'm not kept isolated from anybody. He's a little crazy in his own way - we argue about stuff, just like anybody else would, but it is nothing - nothing - nothing ... George is somebody I can call human, you know. The other "thing" [her abuser] ... I don't know what it was. I don't know what kind of species. I don't understand it ...but you know George can [converse] with my family and if I go out ... now this is something I never got to do, I can go out with my friends on the weekend and he's at home on Saturdays or Sundays. I can leave all my kids there and I'm gone. I don't have to come back because he buys a pizza. I don't have to feel like, if I come home, I'm going to be kicked in the butt or beat up or jumped on or ... No ... No ... No."

Rachel told me, during her interview, that she, also, enjoyed a very happy, non-abusive relationship with her new partner, Tommy. She described how, even their short-term breakup, led to her self-transformation and independence, which, eventually, sparked a total commitment to one another. After knowing each other for thirteen years, most of this time, living together, they are planning to get married, sometime soon,

> "I needed to show myself that I could take care of myself - that I could be on my own - that I didn't need a man there to take care of me. I was feeling good about myself [after the breakup] and then Tommy decided he wanted to come back and I thought, "You know what - I don't want you to come back. I was finally able to say, no. I was so proud - it was like a big deal to me, "No - I'm not

going to be like this little toy you can call, whenever you're feeling horny or feeling lonely' And when I finally started saying "No" is when I finally started getting this strength and stuff. I think right after that Tommy started realizing something. I don't know what, but he finally started realizing something about me and he started sending flowers to my work and calling me up at my job. And Tommy - he's a wonderful, wonderful guy - and my two boys. These are really big things and just being a family - being normal - I guess, you know, in general, you know - "I'm okay - regardless, you know."

Rachel, Betty, and Christine, articulated to me the substantial benefits of having new, non-abusive partners in their lives with whom they could enjoy the highly valued tradition of family connection and support. Having a loving, committed relationship with a man, and being able to provide a father for their children, provided these survivors with the perception they were protected and safe, but also "normal" again. For these women having a non-abusive mate also meant that their children could benefit, and have a "normal" life, too. Having a normal life was described by women in terms of, not only lack of abuse, but also, as increased personal happiness (see Chapter 4: Mastery).

Failure To Recreate Family

Other long term survivors had tried to create, one or more, serious, partnerships with new men, after leaving their abusers, and found their new relationships to be unsuccessful. These repeated failures, *even with non-abusive mates*, seemed to compound the survivors' negative feelings. Sometimes, women would express to me, a deep sense of loneliness, resignation, discouragement and, even despair about their ability to have a "normal" or "real home". This was particularly true for women who had been victims of child abuse. For instance, Mary Ann, after becoming "Disabled Student of the Year", quit college when she fell in love with her new, non-abusive boyfriend named Bill. He was a military officer, whom she still referred to, as "the love of her life".

Mary Ann described Bill as a handsome, understanding man, who, like she, had accumulated many years of sobriety. According to her, their relationship was "perfect". At least, it seemed to be, at first. Mary Ann left college so that she could devote more attention to Bill's needs, and to her new "household responsibilities". She carefully prepared three home-cooked meals a day for Bill, until he went overseas. After he left, she became very active at the local military base; she would soon be accepted as a member of the Navy Wives Club - despite the fact that she and Bill were not legally married. Mary Ann was very happy - she was "doing right", and that a good, sober, "normal man" had actually fallen in love with her. Even her mother and her sister, had finally accepted her relationship with a man,

> "Oh, they loved Bill. They worshipped the ground Bill walked on - that's the only time in my whole life that my family really accepted me as being part of the family, I guess. Bill was military. He was dependable and he wasn't on drugs, and he was good to my kids and he was good to me - and he wasn't beating me up. It was a dream come true."

Sadly, Bill broke up with Mary Ann, right before he returned from overseas. Her entire world collapsed, and continued to disintegrate, for months afterward. She struggled, at first, even to simply get out of bed in the morning, and to get out of the additional debt she had incurred, because of excessive long-distance phone bills, and overseas shipping costs. She proudly assured me that, despite her heartbreak, she still managed to remain sober, for another thirteen years. Mary Ann never returned to college; instead, she began devoting all of her energy and meager financial resources to her adult children and grandchildren. Later, she returned to work for awhile, pushing herself to catch up on bills, and to gather the money she so desperately needed for ongoing medical and living expenses. However, her chronic back pain began to worsen, causing her to rely on more pain medication, just to "keep going". When additional back surgery became necessary for Mary Ann, she spent months, in a full-body cast, disabled from work again, and plummeted into a deep depression. After her adult children left home, she started drinking again. During our final interview session, Mary Anne described herself as "having no one" and spoke, frequently, of feeling suicidal. She was not interested in trying therapy again, and shared with me, the deep loss of hope and strength she felt,

> "I just don't have the strength - to go through all it
> would take to tell my whole goddamn life story again. I
> just can't do it."

Mary Ann was refusing to attend any more A.A. meetings, and expressed deep shame for having failed to "stay sober" one more, humiliating time. With only her income from disability to rely upon, she was also facing eviction at the time of our interview. She was trying to get her doctor's approval for a morphine implant, in hopes of safely controlling the back pain she had suffered for over 35 years, as a result of her husband's assault. She wanted to go back to work, but was terrified of losing her disability payments, and, perhaps, suffering, another medical setback; then, she would have no income at all. She was also stressed over the money she still owed for educational loans. Despite her earlier financial investment in college, Mary Ann still needed additional tutoring in math in order to finish her college degree,

> "My back is still screwed up to this day. Three surger-
> ies, and I have been on pain medication of one kind or
> another from Darvon to Darvocette to Vicodin *and* alco-
> hol to kill the pain, and it still wasn't killing the pain.
> Now, I have osteoarthritis, and it's not just physical
> pain, nerve pain - it's mental pain, emotional and de-
> pression. I'm alone all the time now, but even when the
> house was full of kids and grand kids, I was still alone. I
> had nobody of my own. You know, you can be alone in a
> crowd full of people. You can be more alone in a crowd
> than you can by yourself. [I]t's like everybody else had a
> partner. My kids had a partner - even the babies had
> partners ... and I always hated family functions because
> I was always the one that didn't have anybody."

Mary Ann still blamed herself, and her worsening disabilities for what she perceived of, as her failure to provide a stable home and family for herself and her children,

> "My mother would always tell me, 'Whatever you do, don't tell him about any of your medical problems - because no man wants to be around a woman that's got all those medical problems.' In all honesty - in all fairness to him - that probably had a lot to do with him leaving me - and I can't say I really blame him. But, the kids blamed me - "If I hadn't done this" - "If I hadn't done that" … because they both looked at him with love and respect and loved him more than they did their own Dad."

Yvonne, like Mary Ann, tended to blame herself for, what she believed to be, her own failure to "make a relationship work". Her outward independence and resolve to avoid new relationships and any reliance on a man, was tempered with deep regret about her three failed marriages. She particularly lamented the failure of her last marriage – her husband had always been very verbally abusive to her, but never physically abusive. By the time Yvonne and I had the opportunity to talk together, she had already decided she was close to completely giving up on men,

> "Well, eventually you have to say the hell with it. If the guy likes me - fine. If he doesn't - Hell with him too, because I figure someday … [M]aybe God wants me to be alone. Maybe there's a reason, I don't know. Maybe there's a reason I went through all that. Maybe I liked the game. I don't know all the reasons I went through all that hardship, but I did - and now it's behind me."

Yvonne still appeared conflicted to me, about her resolve to avoid falling in love again. At times, she still expressed what seemed to be a deep yearning for having what, being happily married, still symbolizes to so many women,

> "If they [her ex-husbands] had been decent, we would

have been trying ... if they weren't assholes, everything would have been reversed. We would have been together - first or second husband - whichever one, and then I wouldn't be in this mess. The kids ... everything would have been the way it's supposed to be - or should be - or - you know - what we all think when we get married ... nice - a home for your family. There's some women ... they're so damn lucky - they piss me off these women - they're so lucky. They have husbands that give them their whole check and, you know - he might cheat on them, but they're still there with them. They're not giving up their wife. You know ... Security ... Be proud of what you have. You know, 'Look - My husband does this ...,' or ... 'Oh, my wife says this ...,' or 'Oh - my husband's coming home!' Just the sound of 'my husband' ... it's nice, you know ..."

The long-term experiences of both Mary Ann, and Yvonne, seemed to show that several unsuccessful attempts to recreate their ideals of what a "family," should be like - and to provide a devoted father for their children, meant failure to them. It created, in them, a sense of disenchantment, melancholy, confusion, and pain. Mary Ann, on one hand, had enjoyed tremendous success in many areas of her life, before she met Bill. She was even optimistic, at times, that she had finally broken her lifelong cycle of abuse, addiction, mistakes, and shame. She was helping others to succeed, too. However, after her relationship with Bill failed, she descended into a downward spiral of negative self-evaluation, depression, and self-destructive behavior, again. Although, when we talked, she was afraid to attempt a new relationship with a man, again, Mary Ann still yearned for the companionship and connection that being part of a close nuclear and extended family provides. In Yvonne's case, her prior failed marriages had also caused her to become extremely cautious about entering into a relationship with a man again. Yet, for all of her determination, she still expressed a deep yearning for the respectability and support that she perceived a successful marriage could provide for her, and for her children.

Good Mothers • Bad Mothers

Survivors of domestic violence typically express ongoing concerns about their relationships with their children. Setting a good example, becomes important to mothers, so that children do not repeat the destructive patterns, and violent behaviors, they may have witnessed in the home. Some women, after they leave, discover that children can be profound sources of support in a mother's life, so they may fear the loss of a good, closely connected relationship with them (Hoff 1990). Two survivors I spoke with stated they actually received the *most* overall support from their children. All of the long term survivors placed a very high value on relationships with their children, and on the image they held of themselves as mothers. Successful motherhood provided women with the opportunity to recreate and reconstruct a "family" outside of the traditional social model we have come to expect. When survivors were appreciated as empowered, single mothers, and effective heads of household, their self image was enhanced. Self-evaluation also was heightened, if a mother was to maintain a good relationship with her children, even though her relationship with their father had failed. Having support from family of origin, helped some of the women I spoke with, become more empowered, as mothers, due to the availability of added material, as well as emotional support. In some cases, they were able to receive needed assistance with ongoing childcare needs. Devera, for example, had loving parents who took full-time, 24-hour care of her children, during the years when her husband's abuse worsened, until she could finally escape him. The eight survivors who benefited from full or partial family support also tended to express fewer apprehensions about their children's' futures. They enjoyed close relationships with their adult children, as well as with their minor sons and daughters. Their children's presence and support was particularly important to a feeling of happiness and emotional well being. When we spoke, Devera was enjoying a very close relationship with her adult son. She was also proud to explain to me, at length, how her adult daughter had become an actual role model for her, as well as a source of continual, reliable support,

"My son called - he's getting his pilot's license in June - and this is my daughter and her fiancé. He doesn't do badly, let me tell you - he golfs everyday. They were engaged on the beach in Jamaica, when he proposed. Oh... and I love the way they argue - like my mom and dad. They know how to disagree. So it's like my daughter didn't settle - and it's like mommy won't settle, because I can be by myself for the rest of my life. And when I get weak or depressed, I'll send my daughter an e-mail, "Well Mom is feeling this way or that way" and that phone will ring so fast and she'll say, "What's wrong, Mama?" - And she says, "Mom, It'll be okay - you know everybody has those bad days, but you'll be all right. Just keep focused - just keep focused."

In contrast, women, with non-supportive families tended to experience more problems, as parents over the long term. This group of women, also, tended to undergo more financial and emotional strains as single parents. They did not dare risk leaving their children in the care of their own parents, while they worked, because of their own childhood abuse. Mothers who had no support from their family of origin, pseudo family or from a new partner also expressed greater apprehension about their children's well-being. They expressed regret for what they thought was their failure to provide a "real family" for their children. It is important to recognize that three women in this group had lost custody of their children after they left their abusers. Ellen, who was earlier self-described as the "Earth Mother" had broken ties with her family many years before she left her abuser and explained to me that her own childhood abuse played a significant part in her decision to give her husband custody. According to her, the abuse from her mother, husband and later losing her children, had greatly contributed to her struggle with alcoholism. Although, she had become a very accomplished woman, tears still flowed when she talked about her children, whom she had not seen for many years,

"He had living parents, living grandparents, living aunts

and uncles - my children would grow up with cousins. I had a very psychotic, neurotic, bitter mother. When my son was born, she said to me, "I can't wait until he's big enough to hit - he's only going to grow up to be a man." I didn't want my son around her. My twin brother died when we were 3 months old; he was buried with a cast on his arm. So, the domestic violence is something that we know is generational, and when you're raised with it ... [I] didn't know how to be a mother. I was so afraid I would do to my kids what was done to me - and I've paid a very, very high price. I haven't seen my kids in 19 years - it will be 20 in October ... and this is the one thing that is hard for me. I've gotten over the domestic violence ... I'll never get over having my kids yanked from me!"

Two other survivors had also lost their children after failed heroic attempts to maintain custody. They reluctantly attributed the loss to their own poverty, disability, and/or drug addiction, often the result of their repeated prior childhood and partner abuse. Janice, who said she was never supported by her family, had struggled with a chronic drinking problem since she was fourteen years old. Then, she started experimenting with other drugs after her mother committed suicide and her own father, soon afterward raped her. After Janice left her first abusive husband, she became sober, and struggled to take care of her children for fourteen years, without any child support. She started her own day-care center business, taught Sunday School, and was frequently referred to as the "Kool-Aid Mom", because of her very active involvement in school and community. After her second abusive marriage ended, Janice began drinking again, and one afternoon slapped her daughter for refusing to get dressed for school. She had never hit her children before and her actions that morning made her fear that she was having a nervous breakdown. She asked her minister for an emergency mental health screening, and she asked a friend to watch the children that evening so she could take a break,

"I didn't think I'd hit her again or anything. I just

didn't want her to be around me for awhile, because I'd never hit my kids before and I didn't know why I did it. It was too much for me to handle. I told the doctor exactly what I'd been going through and he said it was all stress related and that I should be able to be with my kids. But she [her 8 year old daughter] told the teachers, "My mom tried to kill me" and that's when I lost them both. Yeah, I lost them both after that. I lost my kids that day. Oh God! I wanted to die. I thought I was dying. I went into like a catatonic state - I didn't eat drink – talk - walk. I couldn't do anything. "

Since losing her children, Janice had attempted suicide twice. At first, she attempted to get her children back, but discovered that, with her in-laws' major resources, she didn't stand a chance. Still determined, she became a model resident at the alcohol recovery home where she resided for four months, then, became Manager of a local restaurant. However, long hours at her new job left Janice fatigued, stressed, and, still, painfully alone, without her children to take care of. She began to think that her life no longer had any real purpose anymore,

"My kids were on my mind a lot. I was really missing my son. I had my daughter every couple of months for only a weekend. They had me working from about eight in the morning till two in the morning and they put me on salary so they could work me as many hours as they wanted. I did that for a month and then I started drinking, just so I could go to sleep at night when I got home … and it got to be where I was just drinking … and on my days off I would stay in my room and just drink … and finally I snapped and walked down to Sav-On one night and bought a box cutter and a fifth of Jack Daniels. I was determined that I was going to kill myself - that there was nothing for me ... that it was all gone - my kids - my family - and I couldn't get it back."

Ellen and Janice have described, clearly, the enormous pain and suffering they both had endured, due to the loss of their children.

In their stories, we see the impact of how women view themselves, as mothers; we are also reminded, again, of the benefits of a strong network of family support. In both of these survivor's lives, the abuser gained custody of the children, because he had a strong network of concerned family and, more material resources - even though his behavior was not more exemplary. We have also seen that, in contrast to the unfortunate experiences of Ellen and Janice, Devera maintained a very close relationship with her children, at least, partially due, to the loving support and assistance provided by her own parents and siblings. Her family provided consistent, loving care for her children, even during a time in Devera's life when she was absent, and unable to. Because of their non-judgmental, committed, and unconditional love and support, Devera was able to enjoy respect and affection, from her minor, and later, her adult children, along with the support of many extended family members.

Children Repeating The Abuse Cycle

Most of the long term survivors, with no support from family, managed despite this disadvantage, to remain the primary custodians of their children. They still experienced ongoing problems, being able to provide, sufficiently, for their children's material and emotional needs. Behavioral problems sometimes emerged, in these children, which caused some of the survivors to have ongoing concerns. Three women expressed fear that their own adolescent, or adult children, were going to become abusers, even though their fathers were no longer in the home. For instance, Yvonne had recently noticed, at the time we talked, that her two teenage sons had already been physically abusive to their girlfriends. As was her habit, Yvonne blamed herself, again, for their violent behavior: for sometimes working too hard, not giving her children enough of her attention, or for exposing them to her past relationships with abusers,

> "My children grew up all messed up because of all the abusive things. I thought they forgot, and they remember everything. They saw a lot of abuse all the time - cops were at our home all the time. All the time the cops

were there. Frank broke a plate on George's head at my mom's house - and to this day, everybody remembers. And he hates him - and now she's like fatherless. Yeah - I see it a lot in Alfred. He will get physical - he pushes his girlfriends around and stuff like that. He has an extremely violent streak in him. We say you're just like your father - violent, you know. Kenneth - I see it in Kenneth too. Kenneth has a vicious temper when he gets mad. It's like when he got in trouble - in a fight with these kids and he took a bat - and that's very abusive you know - and he spent some time behind that. He's very kind and calm and cool. He is. He is. But you push the wrong button, to a certain limit - and he'll freak out."

Yvonne also told me that her adult children, who lived in the home, would not help her with the household bills. She did not understand how they could "treat me this way", because she had always "been there for them",

"I really don't understand - I really don't - they're taking out their vengeance for me, again, that's all it is they hate me for putting them in this 'F – ing' life - that's how I look at it. They hate me for the situation that they're in - no money - no nothing. No future - no motivation - nothing to offer. There's nothing - you know. If I'd have had a stable home - something - they would have had a partner as a father - they would have had a home - like normal - and then, they see their friends - and it's something more normal – and they get mad …"

Mary Ann had already been battered and abused, by her adult son, when we talked. She had invited Roger, her oldest son, and his wife, to stay in her home and help her for a few months after her fifth major surgery. During their stay, while she lay helpless in a full body brace, they decided that she needed "more space". They proceeded to throw all of her college psychology and self-help books away because, according to them, her schoolbooks were "satanic". Their fundamentalist "Christian" beliefs also inspired

113

them to destroy her three favorite unicorn paintings, along with her treasured lifetime collection of Native American crafts – they considered them pagan artifacts.   Those cherished keepsakes, symbolizing what Mary Ann perceived as her own spiritual identity, recovery, and growth as a person, after abuse, were taken from her environment, forever. Then, later, when Mary Ann was able to walk again, the same son, a 6'6", 280 pound man, shoved her, and knocked her to the floor during an altercation over a phone bill. Even though, she readily admitted that these events actually occurred, there was still a persistent tendency on the part of Mary Ann, to deny that she was abused by her own son. She also blamed herself for, what she described as, her son, Roger's "hatred" of her. Like Yvonne, she faulted herself, and her inability to provide a "normal family", as the reason for Roger's violence and his negative feelings,

> "They knew about Jim's abuse. I didn't hide it - they saw it - they saw him rape me. I think he, somehow, had them convinced that he did it because I deserved it - and that's why he did it. When they were younger, they didn't feel that way, but as they got older, they did. When they were little, it wasn't a big deal - but as they got older, it became a big deal - not having your Dad there for the baseball games, when all the other kids had theirs. No father to teach them how to shave - to teach them how to be 'men' - that kind of stuff. Somehow, they figured that I could do everything else. When my lamp broke, I read a book on how to fix it. When my plumbing broke, I read a book on how to fix the plumbing - and fixed it. I was 'Super Mom!' I could do anything - and that's the way they always thought - that I could do anything ... and when 'Super Mom" got disabled - actually everything was pretty good, until I got disabled - that's when the big rift came between us. They thought it was just a sham - that I was just trying to get out of work. They still think that - there's no excuse for me not working in their eyes. They think I should be able to walk on water. The real fact of it is, I

walked on water, as long as I could. And then I sunk.
And I just can't do it anymore. I'm not as young as I
was. I have a lot of limitations - and I just can't do it
anymore - I just can't do it, like I used to ..."

It is important to note that both Yvonne and Mary Ann, have un-
veiled, for us, what could be an unfolding generational pattern of
domestic violence and abuse. Although, these two survivors were
very alarmed at this emergent pattern of behavior among their
own adult children, they remained uncertain about exactly how
they could stop the cycle. We saw that, again, both mothers
blamed themselves for not "getting out" of their former relationships soon enough, and for not providing a more ideal home atmosphere for their children. However, having struggled so hard
for many years just to survive and to keep violence out of their
children's lives, both women admitted to me that they were becoming very tired of even trying to solve the problem again.
Overcoming and repairing the many negative effects caused by
their own past abuse had become, in the end for them, a battle
both women feared they may have lost.

In summary, we have seen in this Chapter, that women with support from family of origin readily expanded their basic support
system to include friends at the workplace, school, neighborhood,
and in their larger communities. Members of these support networks were sometimes called play family, other mothers, or "like-
family" groups. Women *without* support from family of origin,
were, also, sometimes able to benefit from "family like" or pseudo
family relationships, with people they met, after they left. In
some cases, these relationships became long-standing, and led to a
growing sense of empowerment and security. Some survivors also
gained needed support from new non-abusive relationships with
their husbands or partners, and with those connections, a new
expanded sense of family. Some long term survivors added that
having a good relationship with minor and/or adult children, had
given them an increased network of support.

When long term survivors had no support from their families of
origin and found their relationships with new partners later failing, sometimes repeatedly, a sense of regret, depression, and res-

ignation would typically follow. Some, among this group of survivors, expressed deep regret that they had, completely lost custody of their children. Some survivors were despondent, because they had not provided adequate care for their children, due to insufficient material, financial, familial, and/or social resources. Although this group of survivors did recognize the scarcity of formal and informal, particularly familial, support in their lives, they still tended to blame themselves, not others, for their own perceived "failure" to provide a "real home" for their children. In some cases, women feared that their teenage children were also becoming abusers, like their fathers, thereby perpetuating what is commonly called a generational cycle of family violence.

CHAPTER NINE

- VICTIMS OR SURVIVORS?
- WHAT SURVIVORS RECOMMEND

Long-term survivors have described on the previous pages, the obstacles they have encountered and overcome, during the processes of adaptation most central *to them,* surviving abuse. Their unique perspectives and common experiences grounded my emergent analysis of their lives, further enabling me to better understand, what many of them perceived as, a transformation from "victim" to "survivor". I was also able to more closely ascertain the particular cognitive insights they had gained which assisted them to be able to "stay out" after they left. I learned how this information affected the actions women took during various junctures in their lives. Taken together – altering their anticipatory thinking behavior and established patterns of thought - and acquiring a more positive evaluation of self, enabled these long term survivors to continue on, in the adaptive flow of life *that is* survival.

As we have seen, when women with no support from family of origin managed to survive outside the framework of the nuclear family, it was primarily through new relationships they formed at work, school or through other adaptive strategies such as creating their own "family like" support networks. When they became unable to maintain these connections, over the long term, survivors with no support from family of origin and a history of family abuse, were often more prone to engage in self-destructive behavior, or to further isolate themselves from others. These particular women were also prone to repeat incidents of victimization by new partners and, in the case of two women, to being abused by their adolescent or adult children. So, when we reflect on the ongoing experiences and the apparent vulnerability of women who lacked good support systems, it is perhaps, far too simple, to rush to judgment and label them as perpetual "victims". In fact, each of their stories show us, with raw clarity, that these "victim's

117

have been struggling, and "surviving", at one level of "success" or another, for the majority of their lives. It is also interesting to note that when asked if being a "survivor" was different from being a "victim", most of the women I interviewed thought there were clear differences between the two labels. They tended to think of "survivors" in a positive light; the term survivor implied tenacity, transformation, having a positive attitude, moving upward. Cassandra, who had left her abuser three years before, said that going through the process of changing, mentally, from a victim to a survivor, meant developing the instinct to survive, in her words, at a "higher level,"

> "... when you reach the ability to step away from the situation mentally - that's when you can step away from it physically, because you have developed the survival instinct and you want to survive on a different - on a higher level, and I think that's what makes the difference - because a woman who has reached that level - is not going to let anyone put them down ever again."

Devera also described her battle to become, and remain a survivor as heroic. She had finally left her very violent husband five years before I interviewed her. This was only after she spent four months in a coma near death, due to a week-long violent attack on her. She had been confined to a wheelchair for an additional two years and had undergone repeated surgeries in order to repair all of the internal physical damage his abuse had caused. Devera had recently, begun to walk again without assistance. She had also returned to school and described to me the arduous physical, mental, and spiritual struggle being a survivor had been for her. She also spoke about the knowledge and wisdom she had gained by going through the survival process,

> "Going through the process is what builds the character. I think it's what builds the value system - it's what makes us what we are ... that process of going from nothing - that hole - that pit! It's like inching, carving out that next little 'handhold,' or 'foothold' – or 'toehold' - whichever you want to put on it ... and reaching for

that next step ... and reaching more ... that builds it up!"

Devera, also likened being a survivor to being heroic on a battle-field, or as constantly engaged in a war,

> "I have horror stories of the repercussions [of her abuse] ... and I tell people, 'I'm this way because of do-mestic violence.'" And I will tell anyone 'I'm a survivor of domestic violence' and a lot of people will say, 'Oh you're using that for a crutch.' No! No! I'm using *that* as a Badge of Honor! I survived it! And it is something you *have to survive!* It is a fight! It is a struggle! It is something that you have to go through every single day! It is not instantaneous - and *it is not* easy!"

Long term survivors like Devera continued to fight and struggle in many areas: to escape abusers and gain protection, to heal both physical and emotional injuries and to obtain, as well as maintain housing. At the same time, they fought to keep custody of their children, to pay their bills and to solve their own problems. They also created and pursued new goals, along with developing new behavior patterns and strategies in order to avoid being victimized again by anyone else - in particular by the men might turn to for love, assistance, or protection. It is especially important to recog-nize that, even some of the survivors who were not faring as well as others when I talked to them, still recalled with great joy the times they were able to celebrate an improved, or renewed, image of themselves as empowered women and survivors. It is also in-teresting to note that all of the survivors I spoke with, except one woman, strenuously objected to being called a "*victim*". This in-cluded, even Mary Ann and Yvonne, who were both, at the time, being abused by their own adult children. Only one women Cathy, said, confidently,

> "There's no difference to me - a Survivor is always a Vic-tim, too - and a Victim is always a Survivor."

Cathy then stopped for a moment, and added, with a hint of cau-tion and apprehension, "... If she's alive, that is."

Though simply stated, Cathy's remark mirrored findings by feminist Sharon Lamb (1999) who stated in her outstanding book "New Versions of Victims", that *both* terms as well as neither term: "victim", nor *"survivor"* describe the full scope of *any* woman's life. Lamb argued that *all* women, *including women who have not been beaten*, are cheated by the dichotomous labels of "victim" and "survivor". The intrinsically victorious nature of the term "survivor" may actually tend to discount or minimize many of the additional social, emotional, and practical obstacles all women will continue to face, as long as patriarchal oppression continues to persist in all women's lives. For long term survivors and many other women, as long as traditional marriage with the nuclear family remains the predominant "ideal", those women who are loved, valued and protected by supportive families, and later by the men they marry will typically benefit. Their own lives and those of their children will be enhanced in many ways. In contrast, those women who do not fall into the nuclear family ideal, such as single mothers, those fleeing abuse and older women without domestic partners, will usually face much greater challenges gaining domestic and material security. Based on the narratives in this book, even when a survivor found a new supportive partner, she often still faced new struggles, as she attempted to maintain some sense of autonomy, independence, and empowerment and at the same time, avoid mental domination or emotional abuse.

So, as we reflect on the experience of women who left their abusers successfully" or fared better than others over the long term, perhaps *not survivor nor victim,* but instead, *abuse and struggle,* as Lamb also suggests, may be the two common themes in their life narratives, as well as those of all the other women in this book. These long term survivors, along with many others, continue to embrace that struggle today as they conquer new, sometimes unexpected challenges. They remain prepared to fight for their safety and independence, and endure what often is an uphill battle for the well-being and empowerment of both themselves and their children. Women who survive both spousal and childhood abuse have been described by, at least one researcher, as like war veterans (Herman 1997). Just like wounded soldiers, victims of a war they didn't create, battered women heroically return to society, to family, to workplace, frequently unrecognized. They courageously proceed, like wounded warriors to begin new lives. They often endure severe trauma, post-traumatic stress disorder, "battle injuries", struggle, and pain but unlike the oft glorified military hero, the abuse survivor's ongoing battle is usually one that nobody particularly wants to hear or talk about. When she does share her story, she often runs the risk of being blamed, shamed, questioned or criticized for being wounded in the first place.

Many of the survivors I spoke with cried, took a deep breath, and told me they were relieved to finally be able to tell someone their complete stories. Despite their scarcity of resources, they had all still managed to conquer several obstacles and to gain the social support necessary to avoid future abuse and to reclaim their lives. It is my hope that the experiences of these women will offer other survivors and their families as well as members of the research community, a vehicle for further enlightenment, healing, and corrective social action.

WHAT SURVIVORS RECOMMEND

We have all now learned from survivors how they thoughtfully and carefully evaluated all of the various sources of support that meant the most to them, over their long-term experience, according *to their own perspective.* Prior to my own research, there was little specific information about how women did this over the long term, to share with future survivors. Therefore, when I finally talked to long term survivors, I wanted to ask each of them, using their own hard-earned expertise formed "in the trenches" of the domestic violence battlefields, what they would recommend for battered women, as individuals in their struggle toward ultimate safety and empowerment - and for society as a whole. Therefore, as I concluded each interview, I asked for further feedback from each woman about how she would solve the problems that other victims and survivors often face. I wanted these resilient, intelligent, women to tell me firsthand what they and other women really needed and still need today. Several of their recommendations are presented below. Their remarks, and their proposed solutions, should be carefully considered by other survivors, by those concerned others who love them, and by anyone involved in their advocacy, treatment or in making future social policy IPV decisions. Many survivors, when asked for suggestions, emphasized the importance of a person being patient, compassionate, and above all, not being judgmental, when attempting to communicate, understand, and assist a victim of domestic abuse in the most effective manner

On Gaining and Providing Support

"Just don't push them - don't judge them - whatever
you do don't judge - be quiet - listen - don't be the third
person - don't open your mouth just be there as a
friend. Give them a ride. Just be there for them and
don't be an overt witness because I remember my ex
going back and slashing peoples tires and just doing
stupid shit like that - because they know you are close
to them - so they're going to try and hurt you in any
way they can ..."   *Rachel*

"Anyone who goes into this kind of work cannot be
judgmental - they must have an open mind, as well as an
open heart, and be extremely patient. I know for a fact -
every woman who comes out of a battered relationship
can be - and can do whatever she sets her mind to do. I
know that for a fact. I did it. We all can do it, but you
can't do it alone. You've got to have that circle - that
supporting element to help you along - and that's where
our social system fails."   *Devera*

"Give women help – with shelter, with legal systems -
tell them what to do, but show compassion." *Michelle*

"If I had had somebody I could talk to I don't think I
would have gone through the cycle as much as I did. If I
had somebody I could have talked to - a close friend or
relative that you're close to like a sister or a mother - tell
somebody what you're going through because abuse is

like you hurt inside. It's such a hurt. It's guilt. It's physical. It has so many ways of dementing, demeaning your mind, and turning your mind around until you be thinking all kinds of things. It makes you feel shame. It makes you feel unloved. It makes you feel guilty - makes you feel like people are going to call you stupid or like they're going to talk about you. Just tell somebody. Tell somebody ... IF you have somebody." ... *Dorothy*

"A lot of times, when you're going through it, people say, 'Well you just need to get out' - but they just don't understand. It's not that simple. There's something else going on because if you were able to just get out the first time they hit you - you would have gotten up and left ... but even when you get to that point where you want to go - you don't have the money - you don't have a place to go to - you don't have no family in an area ... the kids you have to move them out of school-- it's not that easy. Sometimes a person may want to move from one side of the United States to the other side of the United States and they need the financial means to do so ... there's a lot of things you have to think about, when it's actually time to leave."
Cassandra

On Courtship and Taking Time

"I just think it takes a lot of time. Don't rush into an-other relationship - don't think that you're anything less. Don't let anyone tell you you're anything less than what you really are. "   Rachel

"To be able to make herself whole from this shattered person, women need the time to help heal themselves - to find out about themselves ... for introspection, thera-py - whatever it takes to heal all those wounds from childhood to adulthood. I'm not saying they shouldn't go out and date ... but they've got to learn *how* to date. You don't go to bed with somebody the first time you see

them ... at least that's my opinion ... there are ways to date. There are ways to look at a person to date ... and these women need to learn that - even before they come out and start dating. Courting is a very strong social process that we've forgotten ... You know, have a phone date - that's what I like to call them ... in my mind a functioning relationship between two people is hard enough on its own - to find someone in this world who can go with you in your thinking, or to have a relation-ship that works, two people have to be on the same level – heart, mind, and spirit, and body. That's a whole lot of levels that's got to be the same and we've been running into people who may be pleasing to look at but their lev-els are all whacked, compared to yours. The shelter wants to give you back the authority to govern yourself and that's wonderful, but they also need to suggest strongly that women think about what got them to that point and to think about it objectively - the pros and cons of both sides - what did you do to contribute to this, as well as what he did. And that way, you have a better understanding of, "Well I thought that's the way things were supposed to be." Okay - if you thought that's the way things were supposed to be, let's go deeper and find out why."
Devera

On Healthy Coping Strategies

Survivors also mentioned several healthy coping strategies they had learned over time to assist them in improving the quality of their everyday lives, since they left their abusers. Going to the movies, finding time to "play", visiting a friend, taking early morning walks, or listening to music were some of the strategies women utilized:

"I love it - I love it! And I love the solitude at that time of the morning - the neighborhood is quiet - the house is quiet - it's like magic. Your thoughts become clear, be-cause all the other clatter has died down and - I'm sure there's a term for it - but, it enables you to have your thoughts on whatever ... because there's no outside interference."

Devera

"I love music and for me that's my therapy. It makes me so happy - it makes me calm - it makes me real excited - and I get really high on it - I always have! When I was with him I used to listen to the music just to turn him off - to block the yelling and to be in my world just thinking. Just thinking in my own world by myself. Singing to myself – thinking, 'Oh how do I escape the fuck out of this marriage?' "How can I get out of it?" (she laughs for a moment) It helped me to get out of ... my mind would have to go somewhere and then I would put it [music] on and I would just go into my own - like meditation. I don't know why. It 'gets' me! Like going into another land or something. I don't know what it does. Wow! And I'm like a butterfly! I really am. When I hear it, I'm like 'Oh, man! I'm all happy!' For me - music is my therapy. Something calm ... The kids said 'You like elevator music!' And I said 'I don't care. It makes me feel good.'"

Yvonne

On Social Remedies

Survivors also offered various social recommendations for society to implement that they thought might assist women in gaining an increased sense of independence and help them obtain the resources that they really need to get back on their feet:

"Start a job program for them - help them really get a decent job once they're trained or educated. Because it's hard when you don't have no way - no sense of worth - it's hard, you know."

Yvonne

"I'd refer women to mental health - they can put you on your feet - like me being in mental health - they got me on SSI so I don't have to worry about how I'm going to eat or where I m going to live. I stayed with my husband

125

for a long time, my second one because I didn't know
what to do or where to go."   *Janice*

"They should just listen to them [the survivors] and offer as many solutions as they can, as far as where they
can go to get help, as far as the shelters and stuff. I
think the shelters and stuff do really great - at the shelters they do a lot - they do counseling - to start over -
they save lives - they're doing a lot - they do a lot for
women."   *Betty*

Devera and Ellen's direct involvement with domestic violence
shelters provided them with some unique insights as to how even
shelter's could be more effective in their efforts to help women
become survivors,

"Recognize psychological abuse as part of the domestic
abuse syndrome. A woman does not have to have a broken bone or a blackened eye to be a victim of domestic
violence and she is just as entitled to shelter and shelter
services - and a woman who does not have children, is
just as entitled to shelter services and shelter as a woman with 6 kids and a broken arm and black eye." *Ellen*

"The women had thirty days - some of them don't even
get thirty days - to get themselves together, get a job, get
on the County, get themselves someplace to live, get that
place furnished ... and I was looking at it - it's too fast!
It's like someone whose absolute world has crashed
down around them and you're setting a time limit on
how soon they will get it together. You've got two days
of silence - to be silent - to cry, to weep, whatever - and
on that third day - wham - you're supposed to be well!
Well some people don't work that way. Thirty days is
not enough. ... and they offer the counseling once they
get outside, but once you get outside you're too busy
taking care of the everyday needs. You don't have a car
- most of the meetings are at night - how do you get
there - the bus don't run at night – it's difficult when - it

would be different if they had a bus or a shuttle that picked everybody up and had a mutual place to run the meetings, but they don't. 'You have me in here for thirty days to get me in the system and then you drop me!' It's like, 'Okay - I left the abuser but you have abused me in another way. You told me to leave this man and come out here – well, I need HELP!'"   *Devera*

"It depends on the survivor. Like in this area ... all of the women who come into the shelter are poorly educated they have no marketable skills. Transitional housing is absolutely fundamental for them so that they can go through some sort of training, so they can support themselves. When I separated from my second husband, I already had a job. I didn't need skill training. I just needed a protective roof over my head. I think every client is a little bit different, and I think ... [I]if they were able to bring the women in the shelter into generalized groupings - they need to be in a group together ... so that they are able to form those bonds of support for each other that hold them together, and keep them from running back to the guy that put them in the shelter, in the first place ... but at the same time the counseling that the PhD needs - is nothing like the counseling needs that the person with the sixth grade education from Mexico with no green card needs - they need to be treated in the group as a whole, but they also need to be treated as individual groups with counseling more specific to their individual needs."   *Ellen*

I think personally and it's not an original idea ... they're getting teams together for children who are challenged with a psychologist and a social worker who go into the home ... they have a team to work with the family, and train them to work with the different situations, until the child heals or comes about ... so the team goes from home to home to home ... it would be nice to have a team to come in and provide counseling for the women and counseling for the children 'cause Mom is tired - she's worked all day - make sure Mom is handling things okay. Make sure the children are okay. Let Mom vent - and whatever - and get working on those problems. When she gets to a "level", she can go out into an "office level" - outside for therapy - then that would be a second transition - when she goes to the office and the children go to their own counselor."   *Devera*

On Saving the Children

"Don't do it to your kids - that's what I'm saying - stop the cycle. Try to give your kids motivation to do something. They can do it - they're young. Give them all the power - because no one else is going to do it. I always tell my kids - you're smart - you're young - you have no children. Do what you can. If I could turn back the clock, boy, I wouldn't be in this situation."   *Yvonne*

"If we can get them the first time they come out and get them in a long-term recovery program, so that all the ills can be repaired - fixed - whatever - that is when the success will start showing. You'll see children who are successful students. You'll see families whose basic structures will start to form again - because those women will start teaching their daughters how to have self respect and self esteem. Those daughters will start learning how to look for a man who is husband material, and the sons will learn how to respect women. Maybe it will be in the second marriage - where the women who has found a man who will be an example to the son on how to be a man - maybe - I'm not saying it's guaranteed - nothing is guaranteed - but I'm saying … if the women who are healed can help their children to be healed and teach them - in that open healing manner - how to deal with what goes on in the world … I think it will be a healthier family atmosphere."   *Devera*

PART THREE

SURVIVING DOMESTIC ABUSE: MAJOR PERSPECTIVES,

GOODBYE TO YOU - AGAIN

Farewell my sweet Imposter … goodbye to you again.

Your wore a different mask this time - your actions still the same.

You brought the same failed promises,

the same misleading game.

Non-judgment pledged so quickly from a critic, harsh, and bold ?

A nurturing, warm candle lit? Blown out in anger cold ?

Inviting me to share my thoughts – your interest so intense ?

Then, quickly, what I say is wrong, my words now make no sense ?

Love and lies merge well sometimes … your artful words brought joy -

Then, suddenly I'm thrown away - a trashed and broken Toy.

You said you liked the "real" true me? Then, swiftly cut me down ?

Smiled and pledged to be my friend? Then, discard me with a frown ?

You promised "Unconditional Love," a phantom from my youth -

"Big people" loving "Little me" - then comes the awful truth -

that people try, they die, they lie – that love's a painful dart!

I asked for, first, your friendship. Instead you stabbed my heart!

The broken record plays again -

repeats the same, sad, song -

"Unconditional Love," so right

"Conditionally," so wrong

© M. W. Owens 2013

CHAPTER TEN

WHAT DO EXPERTS SAY SURVIVORS NEED?

D.omestic violence expert Kathleen Ferraro (1996) once observed, "In the 1990s, "domestic violence" represents a convoluted, contradictory discourse that incorporates the contested terrains of sex, love, violence, law and truth … [i]t is a political and discursive space in which emancipatory ideals collide with repressive mechanisms of social control; the legal, familial and social scientific establishments" (p. 78). Competing perspectives collide among concerned advocates, clinicians, law enforcement, feminist, behavioral science and academic communities, about what domestic violence survivors really need. Emilio Viano, in his study, "Violence Among Intimates: Major Issues and Approaches" (1992) provides an extensive overview of many prominent family violence theories. Among those are exchange theory, culture of violence theory, resource theory, patriarchal theory (also called feminist theory), ecological theory, social learning theory, evolutionary theory, socio-biological theory, social conflict theory, and general systems theory. After gathering my own data, I was able to add to this list, family violence theory and network analysis. Some of the data I found overlapped, was in agreement with, or supported prior research. Some was in direct conflict. In this Section, we will take a closer look at some of these perspectives and how they may apply to what the long term survivors I interviewed said.

First, we will look at the more prominent and commonly known psychological and therapeutic approaches to the subject of surviving abuse often utilized by counselors and therapists. These also frequently form a basis for advice in popular books, recovery programs and other "self-help" venues. Afterward, in order to explore arguments, both for, and against therapeutic treatment and social funding allocated for this approach, we will examine the prominent Social Welfare/Feminist Perspectives

131

PSYCHOLOGICAL PERSPECTIVES

Prior findings show that battered women often experience physical illness, psychological injury, or both of these, because of their abuse (Barnett and Lopez 1985; Bowker 1993; Bowker, Arbitell and McFerron 1988; Bard 1994; Celani 1994; Gelles 1997; Stark and Flitcraft 1998; Walker 1994, Wilson 1998). Mental and emotional problems such as sleeplessness, difficulties with anger management, panic disorders, depression, relationship and sexuality issues have also been reported by survivors, both during, and after they leave their relationships with abusers. According to the psychological perspective, in order for women to end abuse, and avoid future abuse, they must correct their own personal behavior patterns in a therapeutic setting. Several treatment methods have been designed to address the related effects of childhood abuse, family problems, destructive behavior patterns, personality "flaws" and pathologies, such as a victim's tendency toward masochism or a "love addiction," that need correction, curing, and sometimes, even medicating (Celani 1994; Shainess 1984).

Following is a brief overview of some of the more prominent   psychiatric and counseling approaches that were available to women, at the time I began my research. These are post-traumatic stress (PTSD) treatment, "battered woman's syndrome" (BWS) treatment, "survivor therapy", and "object relations therapy". I have also included information about some of the more popular self-help and counseling approaches which have appeared on popular media over the years; some of these have also helped battered women and their families.

Post-Traumatic Stress Syndrome

Chronic psychiatric conditions, some of these serious enough to require intensive, long-term therapy, have been noted among some domestic violence survivors. These are acute stress disorder, long-term crisis reaction and post-traumatic stress disorder. (Herman 1997; Walker 1994). According to psychologists, chronic stress while living with the abuser can even result in permanent damage to the woman's nervous system and brain. Post-traumatic stress disorder (first called 'shell shock' when suffered by battlefield veterans of World War I) has been identified as causing life-long damage to both physical and mental health in some survivors. Also called PTSD, this condition is also associated, in many cases, with alcoholism, drug problems, dissociative disorders, homelessness, poverty, and physical damage to the body and immune systems (Herman 1997). Post-traumatic stress syndrome can make work-seeking efforts difficult for both women and men; in some cases, it may necessitate special intervention, treatment, and medication (Herman 1997, Murphy 1997).

Battered Woman's Syndrome

The diagnosis of post-traumatic stress syndrome was followed later by the recognition of "battered woman's syndrome", a set of symptoms first noted by Lenore Walker (1989), in victims of domestic abuse. BWS was later included in the DSM III, as a set of recognizable symptoms, closely related to PTSD. Walker, author of the groundbreaking 1979 classic, "The Battered Woman", through her devoted research and findings, provided a methodology with which to counsel and treat victims. She argued that the effects of spousal abuse on survivors were not only potentially very damaging, sometimes leading to a form of "learned helplessness", they had also become more circumscribed and more predictable. Citing numerous prior studies, Walker (1993) asserted,

> "Since the dynamics of battering relationships have become known, it has been easier to identify the specific psychological effects that can come from living in an abusive relationship."(p. 133)

Her highly publicized approach, also, eventually, became an effective legal defense for many victims of violence, who ultimately killed their domestic abusers (Walker 1989; Sargeant 1991; Wilson 1984). Lenore Walker's work would also provide an unanticipated vehicle for heated argument, later, among academic circles and advocacy groups. Some experts argued that the psychoanalytic communities' tendency to focus on women's emotional "problems" or "syndromes," such as "learned helplessness" might actually have a negative effect on attendant outcomes for battered women. According to Ferraro (1996) and Kurz (1992, 1993) some "therapeutic" approaches can minimize the particular, as well as the extreme psychological and material damage domestic violence *itself* reeks on women and children.

Those who want to help and heal battered women and their families might consider that argument counter-intuitive. However, it is always very important to remember that *any* approach labeling women as somehow already "damaged" or emotionally "flawed" *before* they are battered, may indeed be limited in scope and effectiveness. , Walker later defended "learned helplessness" or "battered woman's syndrome" by arguing that this particular pattern of behavior exhibited *often* by battered women is *not necessarily symptomatic of pathology*, but instead is a *"learned response* "to early and repeated abuse. She also published a guide for therapists and counselors based on her revised viewpoint and suggestions for intervention. She called her new approach "Survivor Therapy" (Walker 1994).

Survivor Therapy

Expanding the boundaries of her initial "learned helplessness" approach, "survivor therapy" combined the principles of both feminist therapy and trauma therapy. Characterized by an egalitarian (equal) relationship between the client and the therapist, it encourages mutual goal-setting activity. It also emphasizes safety, empowerment, validation, restoring clarity of judgment, and the importance of developing increased strength. The importance of education is emphasized, along with increased independent decision-making, and an expansion of alternative survival strategies. In alignment with feminist principles, Lenore Walker recommended that survivors gain increased understanding about their own personal oppression, as well as the larger aspects of social oppression that affect, not only battered women, but also any person or group that is similarly disempowered (Walker 1994).

Object Relations Theory

The long-term well-being and success of a survivor is greatly compromised, if she returns to her abuser, only to be beaten again, or if she enters into a new relationship to be abused again by that partner. David Celani, in his insightful 1994 book, "The Illusion of Love: Why the Battered Woman Returns to Her Abuser," addressed this issue, by asserting that certain types of childhood deprivations, tend to actually guarantee a particular resultant behavior, such as "going back." He argued that a child, when she or he becomes an adult, will continue to seek out partners who recreate a particular type of emotional deprivation that they experienced during their upbringing. This pattern is manifested, for example, by a woman continuing to return to the same abuser, or by a person who perpetually involves himself or herself in similarly destructive relationships. Celani utilized Fairbairn's object relations theory (1963) to formulate this perspective based on the premise that some battered women actually have a personality disorder, similar to that of their respective abusers, which stems from neglectful abusing parents.

Object relations theory (1963) is of particular interest to symbolic interaction theorists (see Chapter 11) because of shared concepts about the mind's ability to create objects or symbols. The mind (as both object relations and symbolic interaction theorists believe) develops sentiments or displays emotions because of interaction with these "objects". Celani explains that abused women, having lost their "bad object" parents, remain, symbolically and emotionally tied to them, by recreating relationships with new mates that possess particular, similar, emotional characteristics. The batterer's "bad object" characteristics, therefore, enable the woman to perpetually re-experience earlier interactions with the "bad object" parents. These habitual patterns make some women prone to repeat relationships with the same type of abusive man, again and again.

According to Celani, a survivor can improve, if assisted, through long-term talk therapy, to undergo the process of differentiation, introjections, and integration that she did not finish in childhood, and, as a result, become able to stop repeating the same old, self-destructive patterns. The overall value of Celani's (1994) model, in contrast to Lenore Walker's approach and other clinicians, may be in his intense focus on the *absolute importance of a young child's early experiences in life*. Celani argued that the number

135

one determinant affecting society's failure to end domestic violence in his words is "… the culture's unbelievable blindness to the long-term effects of abusive or neglectful childhoods". Celani further asserts that, during interaction with his patients, he has, many times, discovered the following,

> "In fact, the focused attention, concern, and acceptance of the patient's real self that occurs in six hours of therapy, often provides more attention, concern, and acceptance than the patient has experienced during all her years of childhood"(Celani, p. 191).

Celani (1994) predicted that, if everything progresses well in a committed doctor-client relationship, an effective restructuring of the survivor's ego can happen within three to five years. However, as an expert, he was also quick to admit that the task is often, both overwhelming, and unfortunately unavailable, both *to the therapist*, and *for the abuse victim*. Therapy is financially prohibitive for most victims, and there are not enough skilled therapists possessing the patience and the required expertise to provide this type of effective long-term talk therapy treatment for clients. Celani concludes his outstanding book with optimism that the compassion and knowledge he has gained over the years and shared will lead to new social policies and expanded treatment methods. At the same time, he remained very guarded, blaming social policies which protect parental rights, which can sometimes lead to a lack of adequate social intervention (1994):

> "It is somewhat paradoxical that I have developed a treatment plan for severe character disorders that includes battered women, only to conclude that it is an enterprise ultimately doomed to failure. My opinion is based on the bedrock reality that the vast majority of abused women will never get a fraction of the specialized help that they require to restructure their damaged sense of self. The notion that we can solve a problem like battering by "repairing" each individual that is afflicted by abuse, without rectifying the underlying

> social problems, ignores everything we know
> about the conquest of similar human dilemmas ...
> large scale social change has to occur so that socie-
> ty no longer 'manufactures' thousands and thou-
> sands of victims and perpetrators each year." (p.
> 206)

Author's Note: It is my own opinion as a victim a domestic violence survivor and shelter worker, as well as a social researcher
that many victims of abuse could greatly benefit from David
Celani's particular therapeutic approach. I gained tremendous
benefits from the ten years I was fortunate to spend with one
highly competent, young therapist, who managed to "re-parent"
me and to literally help me to rebuild my life. However, as Celani
(1994) has astutely observed, the majority of women who are affected by domestic violence are unable to benefit from this form of
specialized long term therapy for a variety of reasons. Among
these are poverty, lack of adequate time, lack of child care, lack of
transportation; also insufficient health coverage and a lack of
skilled therapists.

Self-Help Books and Talk Shows

As stated earlier, Survivor Chronicles, along with self-help solutions have now become a common topic of discussion on talk
shows (see Chapter 2). For those who cannot afford or access professional therapy, experts in both therapeutic and recovery communities have made available a proliferation of self-help books, in
the popular media, written to help victims end the cycle of abuse
in their lives. Beverly Engel's book, "The Emotionally Abused
Woman" (1992) stressed recovery through the formulation of
healthy boundaries. In "Men Who Hate Women and the Women
Who Love Them" (1987) Susan Forward (who was the late Nicole
Brown Simpson's therapist), introduced a new type of therapy
designed to correct what she called an obsessive "savior" or "res-
cuer" complex (1987). Other approaches have been modeled on
the Alcoholics Anonymous or "Recovery" model (Ackerman and
Pickering 1995). Several other self-help books are modeled on a
more holistic, spiritual or healing approach, such as those written

by my highly venerated and respected sister-mentor-survivor, Iyanla Vanzant; "Yesterday, I Cried (1998), is just one of the many, very helpful, books, workbooks, audio-books, and CD compilations she has created for women.

What Some Critics Say

Some argue, as noted earlier in this Chapter, that all battered women do not *necessarily* suffer from long-term "problem" "pathology, or behavioral patterns of "helplessness" or "weakness" that needs to be cured or improved. They insist that when the psychiatric communities focus on the woman's flaws, a very important fact is ignored. According to these experts, the real truth is - that many victims of domestic violence are actually healthy, "normal", successful, happy, even *very powerful*, women - *until* they are beaten or abused. This argument gained prominence when segments of feminist and domestic violence communities began to challenge renowned expert, Lenore Walker's initial observation (also discussed earlier in this Chapter) of particular behavior patterns that she observed to exist in many battered women (Walker 1989, Bowker 1993). These critics of Walker's "learned helplessness" approach argued, that, due to her focus on victim "pathology", a minimum of social and material resources were being made available for battered women at that time. As a result, a debate arose about the actual causes of domestic violence, the appropriate attendant social solutions, and treatment approaches. The debate continued throughout the final decade of the twentieth century, when I began my research. This leads to a group of somewhat different expert perspectives, which are the Social Welfare and Feminist Perspectives.

SOCIAL WELFARE & FEMINIST PERSPECTIVES

In "Battered Wives" (1976, 1981), Del Martin's explosive book, an expose of violence in marriage, the feminist perspective on spousal abuse first captivated a large audience of readers. In this groundbreaking book, the author named powerful, overarching social forces that have historically enabled violence against women: patriarchy and traditional male privilege. According to Martin, those traditional powers have also affected society's failure to provide adequate treatment and support for women after they leave abusers. Many experts still support Martin's thesis, emphasizing that it is *still women* that are foremost, and the victims of *men's* violence. Some have even argued that the new IPV "mutual violence" or "female on male" violence focus has diverted attention and funding from desperately needed resources from the majority of *real* victims - *who are still primarily women* and their children (Ferraro 1996; Yilo 1993; Kurz 1992, 1993). Some also fear that too much attention to increased funding for police and legal deterrence measures, also largely ignores the other long-term social problems faced by battered women *after they leave* (Ferraro 1996).

The solution for abused women from the feminist perspective is more peer support and large-scale social transformation. Survivors over the long term will need ongoing shelter for themselves and their families which begs expansion of the current domestic violence shelter system, more affordable housing, good day-care facilities (and expanded evening and night childcare). Also essential for survivors is fair pay, adequate health care coverage, better enforcement of child support orders and more career planning and educational assistance. Because of these over-arching social forces and needs, feminists are generally cautious about psychiatric or therapeutic solutions. Although "talk therapy" and other treatments can be very helpful and well-intentioned, feminist advocates fear that battered women could be further pathologized, objectified and ultimately disempowered, if they are typically viewed as having a "disorder" or "sickness" that needs treatment. This view parallels Bowker's (1993) counter-argument to Lenore Walker's theory of "learned helplessness", that a "battered woman's problems are social, not psychological"

The Survivor Theory

The "Survivor Hypothesis" was introduced by Edward Gondolf and Ellen Fisher in their book "Battered Women as Survivors" (1988). They found that battered women really *can* become survivors, but that they are often thwarted in their courageous attempts by *both* social and structural constraints. Gondolf and Fisher created the "Survivor Theory", after uncovering what they believed was a condition of "learned helplessness". However, surprisingly, it was *not* manifested in women, as some psychologists had suggested, but instead, by the formal social support systems who should have been helping and providing for women and families. Countering Lenore Walker's theory of battered women as "helpless," they pointed accusing fingers, at the lack of actual social resources, such as shelter, childcare, legal assistance and other necessities available to survivors, both when they attempt to leave, and afterward. And in addition to the inadequacy of provider resources and insufficient funding for domestic violence programs, the tendency in some frustrated providers to "blame the victim" for her own state of affairs, can be *very* counterproductive for everyone involved. Often, according to the findings of Gondolf and Fisher,

> "... service providers feel too overwhelmed and limited
> in their resources to be effective and, therefore, do not
> try as hard as they might."

They insisted that most battered women *do respond* to abuse with sincere, ongoing efforts to seek help, and that women, for the most part, *do not* behave in a "helpless" manner. However, most of these women soon discover that their efforts to obtain assistance are largely unmet by society. Some may return, only to be abused again, and others struggle to "stay away", and survive, with very little social support or assistance, Gondolf and Fisher express caution,

> "The failure of helping agencies and formal support systems to intervene in a comprehensive and decisive fashion allows abuse to continue and escalate" (1988)

The *only* effective, long-term solution, according to these experts, is to halt the cycle of societal learned helplessness, and to initiate a new "social empowerment" directive toward the allocation of more social resources, material assistance, and additional overall social support for survivors of domestic abuse.

Social Support: Network Analysis

Earlier, several long term survivors commented upon the availability and overall effectiveness of formal support system assistance from police, legal advocates, shelters, and social service agencies. However, as we have seen in Chapters Eight and Nine, social support for survivors of domestic abuse can also be measured in terms of the survivor's ties, or bonding to available primary groups. These are typically defined as "informal" social support groups, such as family or the "fictive kin" groups described in previous Chapters. According to sociologist, Lee Bowker's (1993) conclusion, after researching several battered women who either stayed, or left their households, but still somehow managed to stop their partner's abuse,

> "… the women who ended the violence in their lives almost always combined effective formal help sources with informal social support, and the personal strategies that worked best for them."

Despite the value of both formal and informal support in women's lives, only a few studies, in the past have been designed to address *both* the availability and the efficacy of these various sources of social support – most importantly, up close, according to the perspective of the survivor herself and those close to her. The following study, which used a network analysis approach, was one of the few I could find which gives us an additional perspective on the subject of both formal and informal "social support"
Lee Ann Hoff (1990) used a life history approach, as the basis of her field study of nine battered women who left their abusers. As part of her research she conducted several interviews with survivors, as well as with over 130 members of, natural and formal, social networks that were involved with them. In her study, Hoff initially hypothesized that the values held by those in a particular woman's social network, as well as their material resources, would influence just how much assistance they could provide to the survivor. In her research, she assessed those attendant factors, along with what degree of a hindrance, or help those sources of support would potentially be. She utilized what is called value

141

and network analysis, in order to analyze the findings she gleaned through interviewing survivors. She also questioned the members of each survivor's formal and informal social networks, about what they perceived to be her needs, and the amount of social support that was available to her.

Surprisingly, Hoff (1990) found that, overall, members of the survivors' more formal support networks, were, for the most part, *either indifferent or negative in their response to survivors' problems and concerns.* Some members of the survivors informal support networks, such as their own family members, stated that they were *not indifferent or unresponsive* to the survivor's plight, but that they still were unable to help, or provide assistance, due to what they said were *"complex reasons".* Hoff also found that some of the women in her study had been victims of family sexual and physical abuse, when they were children. It was, however, encouraging to find that, in Hoff's follow-up study of these survivors conducted five years later, she was able to determine that *none* of the seven women she was able to contact, had returned to a relationship with a violent mate, since they left. Unfortunately, though, several other problems continued to keep some women in virtual bondage. Only two of the survivors had found truly supportive relationships with new mates. Three survivors were in non-violent, but unsatisfactory relationships in which they still felt somewhat exploited. Only one survivor in Hoff's follow-up study stated that she felt healed from the wounds of her past. Four survivors were still seeing therapists. Some women expressed that just continuing to exist every day, presented a constant challenge to their survival skills. The struggle they still engaged in, to remain self-reliant, was also characterized by a perpetual battle for self-acceptance, and for their right to gain social support and assistance. Hoff concluded:

> "Although the women are survivors, the fact that
> they continued to struggle with a myriad of issues
> and problems affirms the view that their struggles
> are rooted in issues and values beyond themselves
> as individuals. Their individual strength is neces-
> sary to maintain their lives free of abuse. But it is

not sufficient to deal with problems of gender violence that are so deeply rooted in our society's
value system."

Hoff (1990) emphasized, once again, the need for more compre-
hensive services for battered women, and for their families. She
also proposed an expansion of current shelter resources, along
with the addition of follow-up services. Ideally, these shelter resources and services would be designed to assess the survivors'
needs for as long as three years after they leave abusers. Also articulated by Hoff, was the need for a drastic alteration in the
American social climate of violence. According to Hoff, the most
important affect of domestic violence, and one that should be addressed far more often, *is not why women stay in abusive relationships.* Society should be asking, instead: Why is it *always
women and children, instead of men,* who are, so often, required
to leave their own homes in order to feel safe?

A PLACE BETWEEN

A place between … the pain of yesterday
… and the empty book, "Tomorrow"
A stopping point, where plans have to be made -
but emotions scream to be set free

I rest here. - I think … and I cry a lot.
I try to take small steps now … because yesterdays
big steps have made me stumble so badly –
so many times -- that I am crippled by my own fear.

What happened to the fairytale?   We built a castle -
so long ago — and it became a dungeon.
Like foolish Knights in shining armor, fighting a war,
we didn't realize, at first, would be with each other.

All the walls crumbled - and now I stand, alone,
on the ruined battlefield …
pinning my little children to me …
like tarnished medals … for Hope … for Love.

He - who I loved so long ago, and liked,
is my Enemy now … and I must face that!
And I - at last – must face the Enemy inside me –
Myself.

Where do I go from here? And how?
My heartbeat will carry me into tomorrow …
and I must make Tomorrow's Victory …
…   Tomorrow's Peace !

© M. W. Owens at Haven House, 1976

CHAPTER ELEVEN

LONG TERM SURVIVORS
A SOCIOLOGICAL ANALYSIS

Sociologists look for common patterns that emerge in both individual, and group behavior. The information I gained through interviewing long term survivors, coupled with my prior research, and education as a sociologist, enabled me to notice certain processes. Some of these occurred when survivors first "got out", and then, seemed to reoccur, later, during the process of "staying out" of abusive relationships. It is my hope, as one devoted to the study of sociology, that readers will be able to enjoy and gain insight what C. Wright Mills (1950) called "the sociological imagination" - the sociological perspective that I value so highly. In the following sections, the survivors' decision to leave and post-exit life will be discussed, in relationship to prior social research findings about the process of leaving an abuser. What long term survivors themselves said, will also be viewed through the application of what sociologist call the Symbolic Interactionist and Social Process approaches.

Getting Out

Focusing first, on the process of "getting out", several researchers have placed attention on how abused women finally became ready to leave. Information for this research was often gained through gathering first-hand accounts, and then analyzing victims' subjective descriptions, of how they journeyed through the process of leaving. Researchers analyzed what happened, as the victim began to think about getting out, and then, what finally led up to her decision to leave. These studies usually concluded with the victim's decision to leave and her ultimate departure. From these findings on "getting out", I ascertained that, when a battered woman decides to leave, her exit does not occur as a singular, sudden event. Kathleen Ferraro and J.M. Johnson in their 1983 study on "How Women Experience Battering", discovered that an

145

abuse survivor instead experiences a "process of victimization", and, then, a redefinition of "self". The process begins, when she, first, feels a sense of turmoil, which then leads to a redefinition of her "self" as victim". This change of perception is part of the reflective process which facilitates the survivor's eventual decision to leave. Similarly, K. Landerburger in her 1989 study of 10 women, "A Process of Entrapment In and Recovery from an Abusive Relationship", also describes a similar "disengagement process". It is initiated when the woman realizes her abuse is not normal, and then, eventually labels herself as abused and then leaves.

In another earlier study, "The Assault on Self: Stages in Coping with Battering Husbands" (1985) Mills also described "getting out," as a slow, complex process, wherein the battered woman experiences changes of perception about herself and about those in her immediate environment. This process, according to Mills, can lead the victim to begin to actively seek out alternatives, and to, finally, leave her abuser. Related research about abusive dating behavior has also shown that changes of perception, along with "self reclaiming acts", can play a large role in the survivor's eventual decision to sever contact with an abuser. Rosen and Stith (1997), in a later study of women's thoughts in abusive dating relationships, described victims engaged in a "reflective process", wherein they finally decide to sever contact with an abuser. This process included "turning points," "objective reflections," "reappraisals," and "self-reclaiming actions". These culminated when "last straw events" or "paradigmatic shifts", such as changes in perception, finally influenced the battered victims' decision to sever ties.

Earlier findings also clearly established that the process of finally ending the relationship with an abusive mate can even involve leaving and returning again – sometimes, many times. Catherine Kirkwood in her 1993 publication *"Leaving Abusive Partners: from the Scars of Survival to the Wisdom for Change,"* described the exit process that battered women experience, as a series of metaphoric "spiraling in and out" events. The "spiraling-in" stage happens when the woman loses agency, or sense of power, to the control of the abuser. This "spiraling in" stage is then interrupted, sometimes repeatedly, by a "spiraling-out" stage, when the woman experiences anger or fear. This process keeps occurring, again and again, until she begins to regain agency and more control over her life and finally exits the relationship.

Staying Out

When I finally obtained the opportunity to interview the long term survivors you have met in this book, who not only managed to "get out", but were, also, able to "stay out" of future abusive relationships, I discovered something very important. Our in-depth conversations, along with my later coding and recognition of similar patterns in their collective life experiences, illuminated this reality: In order to avoid being battered again, and to change old, destructive behavior patterns, *survivors continued to undergo similar transformative processes* to those described by earlier researchers. After they left, survivors continued to undergo survival-oriented changes of perception and interaction. They also engaged in ongoing processes such as striving to achieve goals, and personal growth efforts. Survivors also continued to develop strategies designed to ensure their safety, empowerment, sense of mastery, and peace of mind. By exploring survivors' accounts, I was also able to recognize that this transformative process of change continued, long after the survivor's final exit.

The experiences of the long term survivors I talked to, also extended my earlier domestic violence research findings, by providing, from *their own first-hand evaluations* of, both the availability and efficacy of, various sources of both formal, and informal support that were available to victims after they left, both over the short and long term (Chapters 5 - 9). Formal sources of support such as courts, social services, and police agencies, as well as informal sources of support, for example family or "family like" interaction with significant others were discussed and assessed at length. By examining these with women, I gleaned additional, and sometimes, even, unexpected, information about the actual availability, as well as the effectiveness of these forms of support in survivors' lives, both before, *and after* they were abused. Several women offered additional details about their own personal biographies. I greatly appreciated their openness, and honesty. Even though, as a fellow survivor, I have experienced much of what they shared with me first-hand, their contribution allowed me to better understand more about the commonality of our experiences, as well as both our shared, and unique, perceptions about the support that was received, as well as the processes they underwent as survivors beginning new lives.

SURVIVING ABUSE AS A PROCESS

The narratives in this book also illustrate the long term survivors' understanding and mastery of the process of "staying out" as a carefully "studied survival" in contrast to a behavior symptomatic of "learned helplessness" (see Walker: Chapter 10). We could see in Devera's explanation of "becoming a survivor" and from her own and other survivors' words that this process does not begin nor end, with a woman's decision to leave. There was not one fixed event or characteristic that totally defined them as "survivors" or that defined or guaranteed their success. Survivors, instead, engaged in an ongoing process of self-reclaiming actions and problem-solving or what has been called by one earlier researcher, an "evolution of strategy refinement" (Goetting 1999). Many survivors' ongoing strategies were directed at avoiding future abuse and on improving the quality of their lives (see Chapters 4 and 5). And as they strived to implement these survival strategies, many women still continued to experience numerous challenges such as poverty, housing difficulties, medical problems, lack of transportation, and nonexistent or insufficient child support. Several were still undergoing serious hardships at the time their interviews took place. Some were looking for viable solutions for temporary problems; some women were dealing with permanent disabilities that had resulted from their prior abuse.

Society's structural constraints on these women's lives, as well as their own personal histories, affected the nature of each individual's survival process. For some survivors, external obstacles such as poverty and homelessness became objects to be conquered. For others, they became chronic obstacles, seemingly impossible to solve. And sadly, for some women, the experience and consequences of being abused and hurt by a loved one had not necessarily begun with their choice of a husband or partner. Some of these women had been "surviving" one form or another of domestic abuse and violence for many years, *before* they were beaten by their mates. Many of these survivors had also been sexually abused, victimized as children, beaten, ridiculed, shamed, and/or abandoned by family members. As made vividly clear in their stories, surviving their husband or partners' beating was, in fact, only the most recent, emergent moment of abuse, in the survivor's entire life history.

Self Reclaiming Actions

As stated earlier, survivors continued to engage in "self reclaiming actions" after they left their abusers (Rosen and Stith 1997). These were often initially taken in order to provide real, as well as perceived safety for themselves, and for their children. Issues such as safety, self-improvement and problem solving, also mentioned in prior chapters, will be revisited - this time, from a sociological perspective in order to provide further understanding of their meaning and importance. First, among these, were survivor's efforts toward GAINING SAFETY – procuring a safe, secure environment in which to live and work. The predictable and reliable support of others, in particular significant others, were important elements in this process. This will be explained further, in a moment.

Second, were efforts toward improved SELF EVALUATION, a better self-image, and self-improvement. This was usually perceived by survivors in terms of goal setting, mastery, or achievement, or, in some cases, as recovery from addictive behavior. According to survivors, self-improvement, produced a more positive evaluation of self, and increased the possibility of being regarded more highly by others. The third need expressed by long term survivors, was to become better at PROBLEM SOLVING. I will refer to this as *"anticipatory problem-solving"*, a sociological term used in symbolic interaction/social process theory (Dewey 1933, 1960; Shibutani 1968}. Improved problem-solving and decision-making, as survivors carefully described to me, involved changing some of their own perspectives, interrupting old habits, heightening their

149

perceptions, and becoming more sensitive to clues of possible danger.

Gaining Safety

Without sense of safety, women cannot begin the cognitive processes they must undergo in order to heal and reclaim their lives (Maslow 1968, 1970; Herman 1997; Walker 1994). The long term survivors I spoke with agreed that along with gaining physical safety from danger, the subjective perception of feeling protected, was very important (see Chapter 4). When survivors became afraid, their sense of control became jeopardized, and the immediate environment seemed highly unpredictable. As a result, some women said they tended act impulsively or "not think things out". Conversely, survivors' problem-solving abilities, were greatly enhanced when they experienced a predictable environment, along with reliable support and assistance from family members and/or community members. Those survivors who were able to reunite with concerned, loving, closely connected family members, who they were already familiar with, were greatly advantaged. Unfortunately, as we have seen, for more than half of the survivors I talked to, this was not the case.

Since only one long term survivor I spoke with was able to benefit from shelter assistance, those without family support, were forced to turn to other informal and formal sources for help. Many found police and legal solutions ineffective, so they sought out new partners in order to feel protected and safe. When new partners were supportive, and not abusive, they could, eventually, begin to experience a sense of safety and predictability in their immediate environment. This helped to create for them what sociologists call a new *"definition of the situation"* (W. I. Thomas, 1951). Survivors frequently referred to this as "now having a "normal life", or as being a "new person" free to live their lives without being abused or beaten in their homes. In contrast, when new partner relationships later became abusive, survivors experienced a prolonged and more pronounced sense of unpredictability in their lives. Early interactions within their families of origin had, already, instilled in some a similar sense of perpetual endangerment. For these women, the ability to effectively engage in anticipatory thinking, and to *"problem-solve"*, which is the behavioral response to a problematic environment (Shibutani 1986; Gaffney 1990) was already compromised. Even years after the immediate physical danger of assault from their batterers had subsided, these women still spoke of feeling uneasy, unprotected, vulnerable, and anxious.

The Role Of Self Evaluation

In order to change in the ongoing behavioral patterns in everyday life, a person's evaluation of self must change. This is especially true after a woman ends an abusive relationship. The new "survivor" identity that most prior "victims" were working so hard to maintain, was strongly associated with a more positive evaluation of self. Transformation toward improved self-evaluation remained critical to survivors, and this changed due to varied interactions with others in their environment. This process was affected by their ability to interact with others. Evaluating themselves more highly, meant that the they were able to assign *new meanings* to various interactions and experiences, and, as result, to have what sociologists call a new, improved *object of self* Mead, 1934) as a "survivor." This could also mean harnessing or "reclaiming" an empowering, favorable *"object"* of themselves, even when interactions with others did not necessarily reinforce that new image.

Many survivors spoke of actually *gaining* increased self-esteem during the process of surviving abuse. Others spoke of being more self reliant, or of finally beginning to really "love themselves". Sociologists would say survivors' potential for strengthened self-esteem, through this process of *"reflected appraisal"* (Cooley 1909)[1], made a critical difference, over the long term. Experiencing a safe and predictable environment, developing a growing confidence in their ability to recognize and successfully avoid

---

[1] Reflected appraisal was described by Cooley as a "looking glass self" through which a person, when considering possible actions, engages in a process of viewing themselves "as if" viewed or "appraised" by others.

151

danger, along with the appraisal of themselves as valued "objects" created a solid basis upon which the survivors could build a new and empowered sense of "self".

Self Improvement, Mastery

Long term survivors have also provided us with their own particular definitions of what a "survivor" is (see Chapter 9), along with accounts of their own "survival" experiences and strategies such as self improvement, mastery, and/or achievement (see Chapter 4). Many survivors were perpetually engaged in *"self-reclaiming"*, goal-oriented endeavors, for instance, being a better mother, getting a job promotion, learning self-defense, or getting a college degree. For example, Devera and Yvonne decided they would never be seen by anyone, again, as "being stupid". We can discern, from these, and other survivors' statements, that the positive appraisal of others, gained through a sense of mastery, or the achievement of goals, can be crucial toward the formation of a new, emergent, and empowered self. When some survivors engaged in *"self-reclaiming"* actions, such as going back to school or joining a recovery group, they were, also, able to gain access to new, and sometimes, previously unavailable, positive appraisals from others. These affirming social interactions were something that some survivors may have never experienced before, enabling her to see herself in a new and more favorable light for the first time.

In essence, positive self-evaluation, and improved interactions with others, empowered the survivor to experience, and enjoy a new *"object"* of herself, as someone who was more capable, and able to problem-solve more effectively and, therefore - a person who could survive, and even thrive, independently. Positive self-evaluation also impacted the *meaning* of the process of survival *per se* for women, for instance, surviving abuse was valued very highly, even in heroic proportions, by some survivors as building character, power and strength. It meant being a "conqueror", a "hero" – it meant victory after a hard-fought, terrifying battle or "war". These women saw survival *itself as* a dramatic symbol or "object" of their success, as well as an opportunity to grow. They saw themselves as taking the actions needed to avoid further abuse, pursue their goals, and to handle their own problems without relying on anyone. This leads us to "*improved problem solving*" an ability long term survivors said was important to develop in order to "stay out" and never be abused again. Sociologists and symbolic interactionists also refer to this by the term "*anticipatory problem solving*".

Anticipatory Problem Solving

Many long term survivors stressed the importance of learning to solve their problems more effectively. For some women, this meant thinking things out, and not making impulsive decisions, anymore. For others, it meant taking responsibility for their own part in being victims of abuse, and then, developing effective personal survival strategies, in order to avoid being victimized again. Their perspectives about the connection between forethought, knowledge, and survival confirm what sociologists refer to as the Dewey-Mead hypothesis: knowledge is power, and the power to adapt and to survive is achieved through the process of problem-solving and anticipatory thinking behavior {(Dewey 1933, Mead 1960, Shibutani 1968}. What I found out, from talking, in depth, to long term survivors, was that, when faced with important decisions, they called upon their past experiences and assumptions about behavior, in order to both anticipate problems that might occur, and to predict outcomes. When survivors did not go through this process, and did not accurately predict outcomes, they often blamed themselves for "not thinking" or for acting too quickly.

Anticipatory Thinking: Predicting Outcomes

The ability to predict outcomes accurately enhanced a survivor's sense of power by increasing her sense of control in the world. Some women had devised ways, ahead of time, to recognize a potential abuser "in the first place", before they engaged in a new romantic relationship with a man. One example of using anticipatory thinking to predict outcomes was clearly described by both Mary Ann and Yvonne by the perceptual process they engaged in when they encountered a "new man" (Chapter 4). They would find themselves immediately reacting, almost intuitively, with unease to something as subtle as the smell of alcohol, or to the raised volume of a man's voice. In these instances, their own experiences may have included being beaten by a drunken man or being yelled at and called names by a domineering mate. As a result, when either Mary Ann, or Yvonne, perceived possible danger from simply the smell or the voice volume of a "new man" in the environment they had already developed an organized survival strategy or *"predisposition to act"* toward him, as if he were actually a threat to safety and therefore, to their new image of themselves or of "self as a survivor". During these encounters, they also underwent an adaptive process that began with this initial predisposition or what sociologists call an *"impulse"* to act, where they would begin to quickly assess and predict, to mentally *"manipulate" all* of the possible outcomes that might result from this encounter. As you have seen, when each of these women described the encounters to me, she was able to step back immediately, and adjust her behavior, *prior* to interacting with him, and before taking any further action. She would review all of the possibilities available to her and then, ultimately decide what to do (in sociological terms to *"consummate the act"*). In both cases, further interaction with the "new man" was ultimately prohibited by using avoidance strategies, such as walking away from him, or leaving the social setting. In instances such as this, we discover long term survivors becoming better able to perceive a potential problem, check their initial impulses to act, engage in anticipatory problem solving, and to exert *"self-control"* over the future outcomes in their lives (Mead 1960, Shibutani 1968).

The Reclaimed "Self As Survivor"

Survivors also used anticipatory thinking in ongoing efforts to maintain and protect the new image they held of themselves as "survivors". The idea of being perceived, by others, *or even by themselves*, as a "victim" would cause them to evaluation themselves negatively. In contrast, defining oneself as a "survivor" was evaluated highly, and to protect this image women had refined and developed unique anticipatory survival strategies *before* potential problems arose. Similar to those of Yvonne and Mary Ann, these efforts were made to foster what could be described as the image of reclaimed "self as survivor", instead of "self as victim". This new "self" was described by some women as interrupting their perceived tendency, sometimes chronic, or even generational, to "pick the wrong man".

Some women had even composed long checklists, containing both the undesirable and desirable, qualities they might recognize in "new men" to minimize the risk of getting into bad relationships again. These "screening" lists were carefully and cautiously designed beforehand both to assess a man's character and to predict his behavior. For example, Cassandra was determined to avoid any man who could not converse and enjoy being with her family. Ellen included the "requirement" that any new romantic interest must be able to describe all the *good things* about his ex-girlfriend or wife. If a potential suitor could not meet these expectations, these survivors had decided, in advance, to end the relationship right away to avoid future problems, or any possible threat to their newly found independence and quality of life. Perceived threats, according to these women, were anything they considered would jeopardize their goals, their self-evaluation, or their physical safety, and, therefore, their newly reclaimed "self as a survivor".

Many of the survivors I spoke with suggested they would use extreme measures, even deadly violence, in order to protect themselves, if they were ever beaten by a man again. For these long term survivors, intimate social environments had truly become potential minefields, where one step in the wrong direction, could trigger a potentially fatal threat, not only to their new identities as a survivors, but also to their physical well-being, in the "life or death" domestic violence arena.

THE REFERENCE GROUP

As survivors went through the daily process of confronting difficulties in their "post-exit" environments, and struggled to overcome these, they also evaluated and re-evaluated themselves on the basis of ongoing interactions they had with those they turned to for support. Interactions with members of informal and formal support systems, during this unfolding survival process, were important to women. Especially meaningful, were those interactions with people who were significant to the survivor, or who represented what sociologists refer to as *"reference group perspectives"* (Hyman 1942). A domestic violence survivor's self-evaluation, and *"reflected appraisal",* according to symbolic interaction and social process theories, would be related to the significant influence of one or more reference groups (Merton 1957; Shibutani 1955; 1962; 1986). The reference group, as a perspective, has been described as an "ideal group" that one aspires to, or as a set of values one aspires to attain, or to incorporate into his or her life. We have seen, many times, earlier in this book, through the interactions survivors engaged in before and after they left their abusers, the transformative influence of *"reference groups",* as their prominent perspectives.

One primary and extremely powerful *"reference group perspective"* for domestic violence survivors is the family. As a reference group perspective, women have, historically, associated the "family ideal" with success as women within the construct of the nuclear patriarchal family (Chodorow 1998; Richie 1996). Even for victims of childhood and domestic abuse, the survivor's dominant reference group perspective in most cases, is related to the idea of a successful marriage, and the approval of her spouse or partner. Therefore, her self-evaluation has been primarily fashioned within the cultural boundaries of marriage and the good *or* bad will of her abusive mate. As Del Martin (1981) stated in "Behind Closed Doors" most women actively reshape their personalities and "accommodate, adapt and adjust" in order to conform to their husband's expectations. Even though many of the long term survivors I spoke with did not experience support from their own families, or from their husbands, they still had tried very hard, to incorporate into their own lives the rituals, experiences and associations they perceived of as representing the "family ideal".

When long term survivors began life on their own, outside of the nuclear family construct and marriage "ideal", their perception and evaluation of themselves sometimes plummeted, *at first.*

Their self-evaluation continued to change, as they rebuilt their lives and the former influence of their abusers became displaced. As new supportive communication channels appeared, survivors became introduced to different *"reference group perspectives"*. Through these new interactions with others, an ongoing process of personal change enabled survivors to develop new evaluations of, themselves (Shibutani 1986). For example, after many abusive relationships, Mary Ann found that she had lost her health, her job, her children and, as she explained, her "identity" - all at the same time. In Mary Ann's case, her prior dominant *"reference group"* of "family" had been displaced and she became very isolated and troubled until she joined her recovery group. Because of exposure to this new *"reference group"* with new affirming perspectives, Mary Ann became able to reclassify her abusive experiences, alter her own perspective again, and gain a newly improved evaluation of herself. Her laudable recovery and empowerment at that time, supports findings that recovery groups can constitute very powerful and effective reference group perspectives {see Katz and Bender 1976 for further information on recovery groups as reference group perspectives).

This transformative process of personal change continued to unfold for many other long term survivors when *additional* new *perspectives* and *meanings* were reinforced *again* by new "reference groups" or when new significant others began to provide empathy and support for survivors. Mary Ann's new sense of "self" as an empowered "survivor", in contrast to her former self-evaluation as an isolated abuse victim, was fortified *first* by her recovery group. Then it was strengthened *further* by her therapist and later, *even more* by her professors at school. She was then able to evaluate herself positively, along with her newly reclaimed *"self as a survivor"*. As a tutor, her abilities were affirmed again and she was encouraged even more through empowering others in a safe, positive environment. This also created, for Mary Ann, an increased sense of social integration and support. We can recall Mary Ann describing, in Chapter 6 that stage in her life as one in which her *"self-esteem soared and everything was like magic"*.

Mary Ann's experience, as well as other survivor accounts of empowerment through social interaction and integration is also seen in findings from the therapeutic community about the importance of support from others in gaining a new improved sense of self (Walker 1994; Celani 1994; Herman 1997). Long term survivors seemed to feel valued and empowered in direct correlation to the amount of support they perceived themselves as having, at various junctures in their lives. This also confirms earlier research findings that for women who leave abusive situations, future interactions with others can either empower them or further reinforce the sense of shame, guilt, and powerlessness they in most cases experience (Richie 1996). The survivors I spoke with, especially those who had little or no support from their primary family group, explained that the most powerful sources of new *reference group* support were those relationships formed at work, at school or in some cases, in new supportive family settings. These affirming relationships were also represented by the formation of creating, or being introduced to "pseudo-family" or "family like" relationships with others.

Reference Groups at Work and School

Work and school settings offered survivors social interaction and support, and increased their oppotunities for improvement and empowerment. The most universal, and readily available, source of support for many survivors I spoke with was the workplace. When women worked, they felt more connected to others and their sense of identity was enhanced. They had a structured, prescribed role to play, at their place of employment, and their self-esteem was often enhanced. Work also provided financial gain and, sometimes, it even offered, what at least two survivors referred to as, close, "family-like" relationships with their fellow employees. Going to college or attending school was also rated highly by long term survivors as a source of social support. Educational settings provided them with financial assistance, validation from others, affirmation, and a sense of hope. Sometimes they also became inspired by mentors, or role models in school settings. At school, they were also often introduced to new "reference group perspectives" which generally validated their new self evaluation as independent, capable and, therefore, empowered survivors. Since the larger society also tends to place a high value on school and work, those people who are engaged in productive endeavors within these settings are often more highly appraised by others.

In turn, the positive reflected appraisal of others that survivors received, both at work and at school, enabled them to evaluate themselves more highly, and to, more readily, situate themselves in their new, improved social worlds. Survivors who were engaged in school and/or work perceived of themselves as successful in, at least, one important area of their lives. Their experiences support the idea that we gain esteem through the roles we occupy, and that multiple role occupancy can lead to increased social integration and support (Thoits 1982; Wethington and Kessler 1986; Turner 1981). For a smaller group of survivors, recovery groups, church groups, or mental health professionals and counselors, enhanced their own sense of support and empowerment, which also created for them increased esteem and an upward spiral of increased connection and positive self-evaluation. In contrast, when talking to survivors I found that those women who could no longer engage in work, school, or other group settings   lacked what could have been very meaningful forms of social connection and support in their lives.

Reference Groups: The Power of Family

The most crucial form of support (or conversely, lack of support), for the long term survivors I spoke with was represented by their past, present and anticipated interaction (or lack thereof) within their own biological families. As mentioned earlier, the ideal of family is extremely powerful and serves as the predominant, *primary* reference group for individuals, by providing a perceptual reality of shared meanings and rituals, along with intimate, deep, longstanding experiences. It also serves as a powerful criterion for self-evaluation that arises, particularly, from those perspectives and interactions shared within primary relationships (Shibutani 1955). Shared meanings and perspectives evolve within each family unit, as the time spent by family members, together, increases, over the years, and as children mature. During this maturation process, images of "self" keep being created, within each family interaction. Through this, a more or less stabile or crystallized conception of oneself as a child, and eventually as an adult as being a certain kind of person emerges. Long term survivors typically perceived of themselves as valued , or not valued, according to this image of self (or in sociological terms, "the object" they had formed of themselves) as a result of the process of "reflected appraisals" that took place during early interactions within their family of origin.

Many of these early interaction patterns, experienced during the survivor's upbringing, also persisted when they related as adults, with their family members, and even after they left their abusive mates. Perhaps feeling, somewhat dependent on their families' approval and sometimes assistance, again, a number of fortunate survivors experienced the reunion with their family of origin as an immediate source of substantial comfort and support. Immediately connected with safe, loving, reassuring interactions with others, with familiar family values, they re-experienced earlier positive appraisals of "self". Survivors who perceived they had greatly benefited from family support were also quick to notice the deep contradiction between the nurturing upbringing they had received, within their family of origin, and the later, very negative evaluation of self they had experienced when they interacted with their abusers. One clear example of this was reflected by what Cassandra kept thinking, as she began to contemplate leaving her husband, "I knew I wasn't raised to be this way – an 'abused person'". Another example of the influence of family as a powerful perspective, was provided by Michelle, whose early upbringing dictated that she immediately leave, after her first husband hit her; it made her feel like a powerless, weak, "little woman", "No! No!" she said, "my Dad brought me up to be a 'Tomboy.'"

Both Cassandra and Michelle had learned through early family interaction that their own self image was not one of a woman who would accept abuse. For those with loving, consistent family support, once immediate concerns regarding their safety and that of their children were addressed, the ongoing efforts they undertook independently seemed to progress well. Returning to their own families signaled returns to positive, uplifting appraisals of "self"with which they were intimately familiar. These experiences encapsulate the ideal of family along with the tremendous power of family as an institution; they also reinforce earlier family research findings that the notion that "self-support" *is* - essentially - family support (Barrett and McIntosh 1998).

As we have seen, when family of origin had been able to provide women with effective emotional and material support in the past, they were also more likely to provide effective support after these survivors left their abusers. To the extent that women benefited from this form of effective family support, they were also more likely to feel safe, to engage in effective problem solving, and to regain a positive evaluation of self or improved self image. Even long term survivors with limited family support, or those who had pseudo-family or "like-family" support were also usually able to proceed toward broadening their support networks. They too, in the long run, fared quite well. Close coalitions created by those survivors with siblings, extended family networks, a "surrogate family" relationship with one person and/or those within what sociologists call "fictive kin" groups were also extremely valuable. In Chapters 8 and 9, we were able to witness up close, the process of family reconstruction, reparation, and redemption.

The concept of familial "caring and sharing" (Barrett and McIntosh 1998) was similarly, expanded in the life of Betty, who explained earlier how she had felt, in the past, having been completely rejected by her own mother and by many of her siblings. She responded to this by re-constructing her own close network of family support, composed of two siblings, a friend who became part of her "family", her new partner, and even, her therapist whom she also referred to as "like family". Rachel, who had also been abandoned by her parents, and then later abused by her stepmother, gained a wealth of emotional, instrumental, and monetary support from the neighbor man whom she called her "Dad". Those other survivors with supportive biological family, or strong pseudo-family, or fictive kin ties, like Betty and Rachel, were generally very happy with their new lives. In contrast, those long term survivors who were without family or "family like" support were still facing many difficulties. Since the day these women were first abused as little girls (in Dorothy, and Mary Ann's cases, over *fifty* years before I interviewed them), some of these women had suffered abuse repeatedly and consistent, effective forms of, both formal and informal, social support and protection continued to remain unavailable for them.

The potential for long term survivors who had no network of family or "family like" support during the majority of their lives, appeared very grim, which supports prior domestic violence research findings by Hoff (1990). She argued that, while a person's intimate family social network may be the most reliable source of assistance, during a crisis, that same family network can also be the source of the greatest damage and assault from a victim's birth onward in life. This was especially true, among women I spoke with, when the absence of family support, in their lives was, compounded by parental abandonment, physical abuse, and/or sexual molestation, when they were young. When this lack of family or "family-like" support persisted during their adulthood, even after they left their abusive mates, the effects of familial alienation were very damaging. To the extent that women who I interviewed were abused, or not nurtured and supported by family, they were also more prone to evaluate themselves more negatively and more prone to make impulsive decisions; these mistakes were often made due to loneliness, financial hardships, intense fear, anger or frustration.

Patterns of repeat abuse, and long-term addiction problems were also more common among this group. Six of the eight women in this particular group were, also, still struggling with long-term learning disabilities; three women were experiencing difficulties with welfare-to-work or rehabilitation programs. These ongoing difficulties substantiate earlier research by Boyer (1999), Herman (1997), and Murphy (1997) who found that social and educational empowerment can present serious challenges for survivors of repeated childhood and adult victimization. Barrett and McIntosh (1998) attributed damage from child abuse as byproduct of the historically exclusionary nature of the "anti social family". The idea of "family privacy" inherent in patriarchal nuclear family settings helped to enable the victimization of these women when they were little girls. Later, when they married and became wives, this same ideal of nuclear family privacy and patriarchal privilege, again, enabled their domestic battery and abuse, and continued to protect their abusers.

After speaking with long term survivors who were victimized, first as children, and then later abused by their husbands, I was very impressed that these women had demonstrated incredible resilience, and strength throughout what was, for many of them, a relentless sequence of painful ordeals. The narratives of these survivors clearly confirmed that they were not "helpless". In fact, they had continued to adapt, and to struggle against great odds for many years. Many women were forced to muster the humility and courage it took, to ask for assistance, sometimes from complete strangers, and by doing so, take the risk of being betrayed or abused again. Sometimes, the stranger would become a good friend, a new partner, or even a "play" brother", Dad", "Papa", "Sister" or other surrogate family member. The survivor's recovery group members for some women, became what has been called a "pseudo family" network (Katz and Bender 1976), which was especially helpful to those who were trying to end addictions. However, sadly in some cases, strangers, new "friends" or, what appeared to be, devoted partners failed to keep their word – again exploiting or abusing the vulnerable, sometimes lonely survivor after promising to help her.

As time progressed after leaving, a survivor's long-term physical disabilities, chronic pain, anxiety, depression, repeat victimization, or shame in social settings sometimes made her more prone to isolation and resignation. In some cases, structural issues negatively impacted survivor's lives such as lack of medical coverage, lack of affordable housing, lack of transportation and the "feminization of poverty" (Scott 1984). These problems, coupled with their own inability to "forgive" themselves for not achieving the traditional dream of the "family ideal" made some long term survivors even more prone to isolation, wherein they further removed themselves from the larger society that tends to ignore - or even blame them for their plight. Some survivors turned to a bottle or overused medication for "the pain that won't stop". The deep frustration, disappointment and sorrow experienced by these particular women, along with the self-destructive coping strategies they were prone to employ, clearly suggested, to me, that they were failing to act in their own best interests, as "survivors." The relative apathy of these survivors during these isolative, lonely periods was also buttressed by a lack of constructive, goal-oriented activity, on their parts. This supports the larger concept which is basic both to sociology, and to symbolic interaction theory - that human nature materializes and thrives through interaction with others - and that it decays in isolation (Cooley 1909).

CHAPTER TWELVE

OUR BATTLE CONTINUES

It is extremely unfortunate for victims and survivors of domestic abuse that the preponderance of competing perspectives may have, in some cases, distracted attention from the practical, and more important issues, affecting victims and families. These are the need for more domestic violence shelters, after-care and housing assistance, identity protection, child care, therapy and help with other real-life problems. Financial empowerment and proactive legislation directly aimed at more social and economic benefits for battered women and their children may be other crucial items that merit our studied attention. The debate among experts continues today, as to what community actually has the most effective solutions for battered women.   Sociologists or psychiatrists, feminists or legislators, judges, police or politicians? The argument also persists about whether women who endure violence, sometimes repeatedly, are "ill" or perpetual masochistic, helpless victims. It is also debated whether "battered men" deserve the same attention and funding that "battered women" do. Meanwhile the resources and actual assistance for any victim or survivor of childhood, partner, spousal, elder, or any form of domestic abuse, now also referred to as "intimate partner violence" still remains scant.

Some experts, particularly feminists, have argued that, since the crime control approach to domestic violence has more recently, dominated and driven research funding, very few resources have been made available to address the actual practical needs of battered women and their children, such as housing and childcare, after they leave abusers. Feminists also fear that the popular emphasis on the "learned helplessness", or other therapeutic models, serves to shift funding away from the other types of material and social support and assistance that women really need. Experts from therapeutic and behavioral science communities insist that victim/survivors benefit greatly from professional counseling. However, we have also seen that professional therapy may or may not be helpful for some survivors. It is often, at best, remedial, and not action-oriented enough, or frequent enough to be preventive on a larger social scale. Therapeutic approaches, such as survivor therapy and object relations therapy have been very helpful to some women, yet as valuable as they may potentially be to survivors, these therapies remain largely unavailable to the majority of women who need assistance, support, and healing.

Expert opinions from the sociological community differ, such as the "survivor hypothesis" (Gondolf and Fisher 1988) which postulates that social support agencies designed to serve battered women actually suffer from "learned helplessness" instead - not the victims, themselves. Although the efforts of those in these agencies may, at first, have been well-intentioned, a sense of chronic helplessness is perpetuated organically within them, due to the ongoing lack of actual resources made available to abused women. The failure of these agencies to help women become survivors in a proactive way may even allow the abuse of women and children to continue and escalate.

There is some common ground, among experts from all perspectives, that the real solution for domestic violence victims and survivors is an increase of additional practical and monetary resources allocated to the availability of practical, material, and effective social support for women. At the same time, those advocating the expansion of these material and social resources, such as domestic violence shelters, safe, affordable housing, and childcare, admit that funding for women and children continues to be difficult to harness.

MY OWN RECOMMENDATIONS
Shelters And Social Policy

As a preventative measure, the need for adequate social intervention in child abuse and/or molestation cases cannot be emphasized enough. New victims - and abusers - are created every day in destructive, abusive, family environments. Education and outreach in churches, schools, and the workplace, should be expanded. Funding for child protective and premarital counseling programs should also be provided within communities at large. For children who are attempting to deal with the aftermath of violence and family breakups due to domestic abuse, skilled low-cost counseling must be readily available to them *and* encouraged. Due to the fact that only one of the women I talked to was able to attain shelter services, it is difficult to determine how the long-term experience of other survivors would have been affected, had such assistance been easily available to them. The shelter environment, like the recovery group, can provide for survivors, a natural or pseudo family support system that is, both, highly effective, and dynamic in its capacity to offer new empowering "reference group" perspectives for women (see Chapter 11) Encountering other women who have also suffered abuse and left provides hope and encouragements. Sharing similar experiences, also enhances the survivor's sense of connection with others, and can help her feel less stigmatized and alienated.

Findings from the psychological community have indicated that dually victimized, addicted survivors can be very difficult to treat (Herman 1997). The domestic violence shelter can provide this specific group of victims/survivors with a safe, nurturing arena in which to begin to restructure their lives. As feminists already know, sisterhood can be powerful, and the domestic violence shelter is an arena where it often flourishes. Specific follow-up services for women, after they leave, with referrals to therapist or groups emphasizing a feminist or recovery approach, can also be very helpful over the long-term (Herman 1997; Kasl 1992). By sharing experience, knowledge, and support with others, survivors can gain a renewed sense of social integration which typically leads to an increased sense of power and more favorable self-evaluation. Being exposed to positive role models who work as shelter counselors, can be extremely valuable. However, with shelters in such short supply, very few battered women are able to access shelter services, in many cities, even for basic emergency and crisis assistance.

Added to the scarcity of shelters, *if* a survivor is fortunate enough to be able to stay in a shelter, given the usual thirty day limit how effective can the shelter alone be for deeply traumatized women and families? Although some transitional homes that offer victims safety and guidance for six months or longer exist, the availability of these homes is severely limited. There is a real need for shelter outreach services extended to women when they begin to live independently, since the post-exit lives of survivors are often characterized by isolation, and a lack of adequate social and material resources. Affordable transportation and childcare services are also needed by survivors and their families, so that they will be able to attend outreach meetings, counseling, job training, and job interviews.

The predilection to serious learning disabilities, among traumatized women and children, also merits our attention. These disabilities must be recognized and addressed, as early in the woman or child's life as possible. Provisions for appropriate tutoring, schooling and/or career training should accompany this diagnosis, so that children, who often respond well to alternative learning methods, can eventually compete in the adult world. With proper attention and treatment, adult, or parent, survivors who have learning disabilities can also benefit from the tools they need to begin new lives. Financial planning for women is also important over the long-term, so that they can budget their limited funds properly, access additional forms of financial assistance that may available to them, and provide adequate support for their children. Achieving financial independence is difficult enough for survivors in general. It is even more difficult for those who are learning disabled, and dealing with the challenges of low paying jobs and single parenthood as well.

Some of the survivors I spoke with did not need professional therapy, or medical intervention. However, the experience of the severely traumatized long term survivors indicated to me that post-traumatic-stress or battered women's syndrome must be recognized and diagnosed, when appropriate, in battered women, and then treated by skilled professionals. Effective treatment approaches for the affects of domestic violence have been presented by Lenore Walker, Judith Herman, David Celani and others, whose treatment approaches were described in Chapter 10. Disability funds and temporary financial assistance should be made readily available to women who are diagnosed with these disorders, since effective treatment can sometimes take years (Walker 1994; Herman 1997; Celani 1994). As David Celani (1994) suggested earlier, many survivors can reap great benefits from good therapy, if only because, within the life experience of some abuse victims, a good therapist may be the only "family like" ally, she has ever had in her life. Many in the mental health community also recognize the drastic need for social intervention and reform. Therapists who work with battered women know firsthand, there are thousands of new domestic violence victims created everyday in a society promoting and glorifying violence, while continuing to ignore the effects of domestic violence and the needs of women, children, and families. Celani quotes Albee (1990) as saying,

> "[N]o mass disease or disorder afflicting humankind has been eliminated by attempts at treating afflicted individuals. Changing the incidence of emotional disorders will require large scale political and social changes affecting the rates of injustice, powerlessness, and exploitation, none of which is affected by individual psychotherapy" (Albee in Celani 1994: p. 206)

Perhaps one of the survivors in my study says it even more eloquently. Devera, during her interviews, placed great emphasis on, both the role of family *and* the responsibility of society, to provide long-term support for what is, in reality, a very complex, persistent problem which is both individual *and* social,

> "I've been very fortunate. I've had examples all throughout my life, which is why I think I've been able to come through this like I have ... but there are a lot of women who have never had an example. They came from an abusive home, and their mothers came from an abusive home. It's a generational kind of problem that they're trying to do a "quick fix" with - and it's not going to work. You can't do a "quick fix" on something that has gone on, this long, in the way of self-respect and self-esteem."

The necessary therapeutic treatment and social measures needed by victims and survivors may seem, at first glance, very expensive to implement. Yet, the cost of human suffering will be much greater, if society does not respond, in a major way, to provide effective assistance and support for survivors of domestic abuse. Domestic violence advocates have, for too long been forced to rely on limited funding, charity functions and hard fought legislative battles for bills that have provided still insufficient support. Shelter employees continue to work for very low wages. Adding to this shameful economic inequity, many domestic violence shelter employees are also past *victims of abuse themselves!* These survivors are highly motivated, as well as *uniquely prepared through their experience and knowledge*, to help others learn, heal, and gain freedom from violence. This army of survivors should be utilized more often, employed by shelters, receive adequate training, and then, they should be compensated adequately for their knowledge and work. Dedicated efforts have been made in this direction both by women's advocates and by domestic violence survivor's themselves. Three of the survivors in my study had, either volunteered or gained employment at domestic violence shelters, after they left their abusers. They were actively involved in what has been called their own personal "survivor missions" (Herman 1997).

I fulfilled my own "survivor mission" through my (extremely fulfilling albeit vastly underpaid) employment as a 24-hour hotline advisor and intake worker at a California domestic violence, shelter several years ago. I answered desperate, urgent calls, with sometimes a woman screaming over the phone, a man yelling, or children crying in the background. I would rush to meet victims, at secret locations, after they had escaped. They were terrified, often with no belongings, carrying frightened children in their arms. I would bring them in, offering a hairbrush, some toothpaste and a place for them to sleep and feel safe, finally, for at least that night. Sometimes the women couldn't sleep, and we would talk together, all night, sharing "battlefield stories", only to be interrupted, at times, by another emergency call from a victim, or from a concerned relative. Through employment such as this, survivors can benefit from the money they earn, and at the same time, engage in meaningful social action, directed toward the healing and empowerment of others, like themselves. In doing so, survivors gain the additional strength and fortitude that serves to further their own healing (Hallock 1998; Herman 1997; Vanzant 1998; Walker 1994). Ellen found such affirmation and power through her work with rape victims at a community agency that served both victims of rape and of abuse. Another survivor, Devera was volunteering at the local battered women's shelter, and intended to devote the rest of her life to serving abused women, especially in those agencies that assist families and children. Betty had also contributed many hours to helping, advising, and peer counseling other abuse victims.

Because of the limited available funding for such agencies, experienced, well-informed survivors such as Ellen, Devera, and Betty, must often volunteer, working for free, or earn little more than minimum wage for their dedicated and, what sometimes can actually be life-threatening work. First abused by their husbands, these highly skilled, competent, compassionate women, are then financially victimized again by a society which refuses to recognize the important function they are uniquely able to perform, both as advisors, and as role models. More funding allocated to progressive programs directed against both child and domestic abuse, that also include in their focus the employment and empowerment of prior victims, could represent a very meaningful contribution toward the prevention of violence and, in turn, to the success of family life in this new millennium.

THE END

 # IN MEMORIAM

REST IN PEACE

To YVONNE

Delicate, vulnerable, yet still strong, vibrant and valiant. After surviving the abuse of three men, so close to her goal, Yvonne still had to fight one more battle. Shortly after we spoke, she waged a courageous war against cancer, went into remission, and was proclaimed a 5 year "Survivor". A year, later, cancer, attacked her, again … though very frightened, she remained a warrior … but was finally forced to surrender. A true Champion, forever tenacious and determined, Yvonne did attain her lifelong dream of earning her college degree, "so that no one could even call me 'stupid' again", shortly before her death. Congratulations - You Made It to the Finish Line, Yvonne.

To DOROTHY

A woman, who loved to have fun, and who always had a ready smile. She loved to laugh, and treated everyone as a friend. Full of joy, and love for life, Dorothy passed from this earth, not too long before I finished this book. Rest in Peace, Sister Survivor! You will never be homeless now, and will never suffer from poverty again. Rest in Peace – and - as you told me, during your interview, God was always there - watching over you. You said to me, "We have the Angels around us that watches us, - and we have God Himself!" Dorothy, He has now welcomed you into His gentle, loving, strong arms - you are finally safe and protected, and no one on this earth can ever hurt, harm, or abuse you again.

CHRISTMAS AT THE SHELTER

I'd forgotten the scurry of little feet
and how bright a child's eyes could be.
I'd forgotten the sound of non-stop laughter,
the magic of holiday glee.

What a sight that Christmas morning
as I walked in the shelter door,
to the sound of children's laughter,
as gift wrap flew up from the floor.

The carolers visited, later that day,
with hugs, and cookies, and song ...
and then I remembered what Christmas was ...
I'd forgotten for oh, so long.

Santa arrived at our "home' that day,
and he hadn't forgotten a soul!
Though our hearts were filled with fear .. and pain,
LOVE entered ... and made us whole.

© M. W. Owens   Hotline Counseling,
VCAHV Shelter: Winter 1988

REFERENCES

Ackerman Robert J. and Susan E. Pickering. 1995. *Before It's Too Late: Helping Women in Controlling or Abusive Relationships*. Deerfield Beach: Health Communications.

Bard Marjorie. 1994. *Organizational and Community Responses to Domestic Abuse and Homelessness*. New York: Garland Press.

Barrett Michelle and Mary McIntosh. 1998. "The Anti Social Family." Pp. 219-29 in *Families in the U.S.: Kinship and Domestic Politics*, edited by Karen V. Hansen and Anita Garey. Philadelphia: Temple University Press.

Bassuk Ellen L. 1990. Who Are the Homeless Families: Characteristics of Sheltered Mothers and Children. *Community Mental Health Journal* 26 (5):425-34

Berk Richard A. 1993. "What the Scientific Evidence Shows: On the Average, We Can Do No Better Than Arrest." pp. 323-36 in *Current Controversies on Family Violence*, edited by Richard J. Gelles and Donileen R. Loseke. Newbury Park, California. Sage.

Berg Bruce L. 1998. *Qualitative Research Methods for the Social Sciences*. Boston: Allyn & Bacon.

Blumer Herbert. 1969. *Symbolic Interactionism: Perspective and Method*. Englewood Cliffs, N.J.: Prentice Hall Inc.

Bowker Lee H. and Laurie Maurer. 1986. "The Effective-ness of Counseling Services Utilized by Battered Women." *Women and Therapy* 5:65-82.

Bowker Lee H. and Laurie Maurer. 1985. "The Importance of Sheltering in the Lives of Battered Wives." *Response to the Victimization of Women and Children* 7:2-11.

Bowker Lee H. 1986. *Ending the Violence: A Guidebook Based on the Experiences of 1,000 Battered Wives*. Holmes Beach: Learning Publications.

Bowker Lee H., M. Arbitell, and J. R. McFerron. 1988. "On the Relationship Between Wife Beating and Child Abuse." Pp. 158-74 in *Feminist Perspectives on Wife Abuse*, edited by K. Yilo and M. Bograd. Beverly Hills: Sage.

Bowker Lee. H. 1983. *"Coping with Wife Abuse: Personal and Social Networks."* Pp. 160-91 in *Battered Women and Their Families: Intervention Strategies and Treatment Strategies*, edited by Albert R. Roberts. New York: Springer.

Bowker Lee. H. 1993. "A Battered Women's Problems are Social, Not Psychological." Pp. 154-65 in *Current Controversies on Family Violence,* edited by Richard J. Gelles and Donileen R. Loseke. Newbury Park: Sage.

Boyer Debra. 1999. "Childhood Sexual Abuse: The Forgotten Issue in Adolescent Pregnancy and Welfare Reform." Pp. 131-43 in *Battered Women, Children and Welfare Reform,* edited by Ruth Brandwein. Thousand Oaks: Sage.

Browne Angela. 1997. "Marital Violence: Battered Women." Pp. 211-31 in *Family Violence Across the Lifespan,* edited by Ola W. Barnett, Cindy L. Miller-Perrin and Robin D. Perrin. Thousand Oaks, California: Sage.

Browne Angela, Amy Salomon and Shari S. Bassuk. 1999. "The Impact of Recent Partner Violence on Poor Women's Capacity to Maintain Work." *Violence Against Women* 5:393-426

Burr Wesley R., Geoffrey K. Leigh, Randall D. Day, and John Constantine. 1979. "Symbolic Interaction and the Family." Pp. 42-111 in *Contemporary Theories About The Family: General Theories/Theoretical Observations*, edited by Wesley R. Burr Reuben Hill, Ivan F. Nye, Ira L. Reiss, New York: The Free Press.

Burt Martha R. and Barbara E. Cohen. 1989. Differences Between Homeless Single Women, Women With Children and Single Men. *Social Problems* 36 (5):508-524

Buzawa E. E. and Busawa. C. G. 1990. *Domestic Violence: The Criminal Justice Response*. Newbury Park: Sage.

Campbell Jacquelyn C., Paul Miller, and Mary M. Cardwell. 1994. "Relationship Status of Battered Women Over Time." *Journal of Family Violence* 9 (6):99-111.

Celani David P. 1994. *The Illusion of Love: Why the Battered Woman Returns to Her Abuser.* New York: Columbia University Press.

Chodorow Nancy J. 1998. "Why Women Mother." Pp. 271-93 in *Families in the U.S. Kinship and Domestic Politics,* edited by Karen V. Hansen and Anita Garey. Philadelphia: Temple University Press.

Cooley Charles Horton. 1972. "Primary Group and Human Nature." Pp. 158-60 in *Symbolic Interaction: A Reader in Social Psychology.* Second ed. Boston: Allyn and Bacon.

Couch Carl J. 1962. "Family Role Specialization and Self Attitudes in Children." *The Sociological Quarterly* 3 (2):115-21.

Davis M.F. And S.J. Kraham. 1985. "Protecting Women's Welfare in the Face of Violence." Fordham Urban Law Journal 22 (4):1141-57

Deed M. 1991. Court Ordered Child Custody Evaluations: Helping or Victimizing Vulnerable Families. *Psychotherapy* 11:76-84.

Dewey John. 1933, 1960. *How we Think: A Restatement of the Relation of Reflective Thinking to the Educative Process.* Lexington Massachusetts: D.C. Heath and Company.

Dobash.R.E. and R. P. Dobash. 1979. *Violence Against Wives: A Case Against Patriarchy.* New York: The Free Press.

Mary Ann. 1992. *Empowering and Healing the Battered Woman: A Model for Assessment and Intervention.* New York: Springer Publishing Company.

Eisikovits Zvi. and Eli. Buchbinder. 1996. Pathways to Disenchantment: Battered Women's Views of Their Social Workers. *Journal of Interpersonal Violence.* 11:425-40.

Ellis Desmond. 1992. "Woman Abuse Among Separated and Divorced Women: The Relevance of Social Support." Pp. 177-89 in *Intimate Violence: Interdisciplinary Perspectives,* edited by Emilio Viano. Bristol: Taylor and Francis.

Engel Beverly. 1992. *The Emotionally Abused Woman*. New York; Fawcett

Fairbairn W.R.D. 1963. "Synopsis of an Object-Relations Theory of the Personality." *International Journal of Psycho-Analysis* 44:224-255

Ferraro K. J. and J. M. Johnson. 1983. "How Women Experience Battering: The Process of Victimization." *Social Problems* 30 (3):325-39.

Ferraro K. J. 1999. "Policing Woman Battering." *Social Problems* 36 (1):61-74.

Ferraro Kathleen J. 1996. "The Dance of Dependency: A Genealogy of Domestic Violence." *Hypatia* 11 (4):77-91.

Fischer Karla., and Mary Rose. 1995. "When "Enough is Enough": Battered Women's Decision Making Around Court Orders of Protection." *Crime and Delinquency* October, 1995: 41 (4):414-29.

Forward Susan. 1987. *Men Who Hate Women and the Women Who Love Them*. New York: Bantam Books.

Fox E. 1985. *Homelessness in Philadelphia: People, Needs and Services*. Philadelphia, Pennsylvania: Philadelphia Health Management Corporation.

Gaffney Marta. 1990. "In Search of the Agent in Charge." Masters Thesis, Department of Sociology, University of California, Santa Barbara.

Gelles Richard J. and Donileen R. Loseke. 1993. *Current Controversies on Family Violence*. Edited by Richard J. Gelles and Donileen R. Loseke. Newbury Park, California: Sage.

Gelles Richard J. 1997. *Intimate Violence in Families*. Thousand Oaks, California: Sage.

Glaser Barney and Anselm L. Strauss. 1967. *The Discovery of Grounded Theory*. Hawthorne, New York: Aldine de Gruyter.

Goetting Ann. 1999. *Getting Out: Life Stories of Women Who Left Abusive Men*. New York: Columbia University Press.

Gondolf Edward W. and Ellen R. Fisher. 1988. *Battered Women As Survivors*. New York: Lexington Books.

Hallock Daniel. 1998. *Hell, Healing, and Resistance: Veterans Speak*. Farmington: Plough House.

Harding Sandra. 1987. Introduction Pp. 1-14 to Feminism and Methodology edited by Sandra Harding. Bloomington: Indiana University Press

Herman Judith. 1997. *Trauma and Recovery*. New York: Harper Collins. Hoff Lee Ann. 1990. *Battered Women as Survivors*. New York: Routledge.

Horney Karen. 1950. *Neurosis and Human Growth*. New York: W. W. Norton & Co.

Hyman Herbert. 1942. *The Psychology of Status*. PH.D, Columbia University, New York.

Jacobsen David E. 1986. "Types and Timing of Social Support." *Journal of Health and Social Behavior* 27 (3):250-64.

Kasl Charlotte Davis. 1992. *Many Roads, One Journey: Moving Beyond the Twelve Steps*. New York: Harper Collins

Katz Alfred H. Bender Eugene I. 1976. *The Strength in Us: Self Help Groups in the Modern World*. New York: New Viewpoints.

Kirkwood Catherine. 1993. *Leaving Abusive Partners: from the Scars of Survival to the Wisdom for Change*. Newbury Park: Sage.

Kurz Demi. 1992. "Battering and the Criminal Justice System: A feminist view." Pp. 21-38 in *Domestic Violence: The Criminal Justice Response,* edited by E.E. Buzawa and C. G. Buzawa. Westport, Connecticut: Auburn House.

Kurz Demi. 1993. "Physical Assaults by Husbands: A Major Social Problem." Pp. 88-103 in *Current Controversies on Family Violence,* edited by Richard J. Gelles and Donileen R. Loseke. Newbury Park: Sage.

Lamb Sharon. 1999. "Constructing the Victim: Popular Images and Lasting Labels." Pp. 108-38 in *New Versions of Victims: Feminists Struggle with the Concept*, edited by Sharon Lamb. New York: New York University Press.

Landerburger K. 1989. "A Process of Entrapment In and Recovery from an Abusive Relationship." *Issues in Mental Health Nursing* 10 (3-4):209-227

Lerman L.G. 1984. "Model State Act: Remedies for Domestic Abuse." *Harvard Journal on Legislation 21, 61, 90*

Lerner Gerda. 1986. *The Creation of Patriarchy*. New York: Oxford University Press.

Liss M.B.and Stahly G. B. 1993. "Domestic Violence and Child Custody." Pp. 200-16 in *Battering and Family Therapy: A Feminist Perspective*, edited by M. Hansen and M. Harway. Newbury Park: Sage.

Loseke D. R. 1992. *The Battered Woman and Shelters: the Social Construction of Wife Abuse*. Albany: State University of New York Press.

Martin Dell. 1981. *Battered Wives*. San Francisco: Volcano Press.

Maslow Abraham. 1968. *Toward A Psychology of Well Being*. Princeton: Van Nostrad.

Maslow Abraham. 1970. *Motivation and Personality*. New York: Harper and Row.

Mead George Herbert. 1934. *Mind, Self and Society*. Chicago: University of Chicago Press.

Meloy Helen Ann. 1993. "Irresistible Urges: The Social Psychology of Binge Eating." PhD Dissertation, Department of Sociology, University of California, Santa Barbara.

Merton Robert K. 1957. *Social Theory and Social Structure*. Glencoe: The Free Press.

Michael, Lee. 1994. *I Started to Say I Love You but Your First Got in the Way and Other Love Poems.* Quinn Publishing, Las Vegas

Mills T. 1985. "The Assault on Self: Stages in Coping with Battering Husbands." *Qualitative Sociology* 8 (2):103-23.

Murphy Patricia. 1997. "Recovering from the Effects of Domestic Violence." *Law and Policy* 19 (2):169-82.

Neuman W. Lawrence. 1997. *Social Research Methods: Qualitative and Quantitative Approaches.* Boston: Allyn and Bacon.

NiCarthy G. 1987. *The Ones Who Got Away: Women Who Left Abusive Partners.* Seattle: Seal.

NiCarthy Ginny. 1997. *Getting Free: You Can End Abuse and Take Back Your Life.* Seattle: Seal Press.

Ollenberger Jane C. and Helen A. Moore. 1998. *A Sociology of Women.* New Jersey: Prentice Hall.

Primezone Media Network (2005). Shocking New Statistics on Domestic Violence in U.S. – In Response Americans are Being Urged to Spring Clean with a Conscience by Donating a Phone and Saving a Life. Available at: URL: http://www.ncdsv.org/images/ShockingNewStatisticsDVUS.pdf .

Raphael J. 2000. *Saving Bernice: Battered Women, Welfare, and Poverty.* Boston: Northeastern University Press.

Raphael J. 1996. *Prisoners of Abuse: Domestic Violence and Welfare Receipt.* Chicago: Taylor Institute.

Raphael J and R. Tolman. 1997. *Trapped by Poverty/Trapped by Abuse.* Chicago: Taylor Institute.

Raphael J. 1995. *Domestic Violence: Telling the Untold Welfare to Work Story.* Chicago: Taylor Institute.

Reinharz, S. 1992. *Feminist Methods in Social Research.* New York: Oxford University Press.

ichie Beth E. 1996. *Compelled to Crime: The Gender Entrapment of Battered Black Women.* New York: Routledge.

Rosen Karen H. and Sandra M. Stith. 1997. "Surviving Abusive Dating Relationships." Pp. 170-82 in *Out of the Darkness: Contemporary Perspectives on Family Violence,* edited by Glenda Kantor and Jana L. Jasinski. Thousand Oaks: Sage

Sargeant Georgia. 1991. "Battered Woman Syndrome" Gaining Legal Recognition." *Trial* 27 (4):17-21.

Schwartz H. and J. Jacobs. 1979. *Qualitative Sociology: A Method to the Madness* New York: Free Press.

Schechter Susan. 1982. *Women and Male Violence: The Visions and Struggles of the Battered Women's Movement.* Boston: South End Press.

Schillinger Elisabeth. 1988. "Dependency, Control, and Isolation: Battered Women and the Welfare System." *Journal of Contemporary Ethnography* 16:469-90.

Scott H. 1984. *Working Your Way to the Bottom.* Boston: Pandora Press.

Shainess Natalie. 1984. *Sweet Suffering: Woman as Victim.* New York: Pocket Books.

Sherman Lawrence W., Janell D. Schmidt, and Dennis P. Rogan. 1992. *Policing Domestic Violence: Experiments and Dilemmas.* New York: The Free Press.

Sherman Lawrence W. 1997. "Marital Violence: An Overview." Pp. 185-207 in *Family Violence Across the Lifespan,* edited by Ola W. Barnett, Cindy L. Miller-Perrin and Robin D. Perrin. Thousand Oaks: Sage.

Shibutani Tamotsu. 1955. "Reference Groups as Perspectives."

American Journal of Sociology, University of Chicago Press 60:562-9.

Shibutani Tamotsu. 1962. "Reference Groups and Social Control." Pp. 128-47 in *Human Behavior and Social Process*, edited by Arnold Rose. Boston: Houghton Mifflin Co.

Shibutani Tamotsu. 1968. "George Herbert Mead." Pp. 83-87 in *International Encyclopedia of the Social Sciences*. New York: Cowell Collier & MacMillan.

Shibutani Tamotsu. 1986. *Social Process*. Berkeley: University of California Press.

Shibutani Tamotsu. 1961. *Society and Personality*. Englewood Cliffs: Prentice Hall.

Stack Carol D. 1974. *All Our Kin: Strategies for Survival in a Black Community*. New York: Harper & Row

Stark Evan and Anne Flitcraft. 1979. "Medicine and Patriarchal Violence: The Social Construction of a Private Event." *International Journal of Health Services* 9: 462-93.

Stark Evan and Anne Flitcraft. 1998. "Women and Children at Risk: A Feminist Perspective on Child Abuse." Pp. 25-41 in *Issues in Intimate Violence*. Thousand Oaks: Sage.

Statman Jan Berliner. 1990. *The Battered Woman's Survival Guide*. Dallas: Taylor Publishing Company.

Straus Murray A., Richard J. Gelles, and Suzanne K. Steinmetz. 1980. *Behind Closed Doors*. Garden City: Anchor Press/Doubleday.

Strauss Anslem L. and Juliet M. Corbin. 1990. *Basics of Qualitative Research: Grounded Theory Procedures and Techniques*. Newbury Park: Sage.

Strube M. J. And L. S. Barbour. 1983. "The Decision to Leave an Abusive Relationship: Economic and Psychological Commitment." *Journal of Marriage and the Family* 45:785-93

Thoits Peggy. 1982. "Conceptual, Methodological, and Theoretical Problems in Studying Social Support as a Buffer Against Life Stress." *Journal of Health and Social Behavior* 23 (2):145-59.

Thomas W. I. 1931. "The Definition of the Situation." Pp. 331-36 in *Symbolic Interaction,* edited by Jerome G. Manis and Bernard N. Meltzer. Boston: Allyn & Bacon

Tjaden, P. & Thoennes, N. (2000a). Extent, Nature, and Consequences of Intimate Partner Violence: Findings from the National Violence Against Women Survey. Washington, D.C.: US Department of Justice. Publication No. CJ181867.
Available at URL: www.ojp.usdoj.gov/nij/pubs-um/181867.htm.

Turner R. Jay. 1981. "Social Support as a Contingency in Psychological Well Being." *Journal of Health and Social Behavior* 22:357-67.

Vanzant, Iyanla, 2011. *Peace from the Broken Pieces*, New York: SmileyBooks

Vanzant Iyanla. 1998. *Yesterday, I Cried.* New York: Simon and Schuster.

Viano Emilio C. 1992. "Violence Among Intimates: Major Issues and Approaches." Pp. 3-12 in *Intimate Violence: Interdisciplinary Perspectives*, edited by Emilio C. Viano. Bristol: Taylor and Francis.

Walker Lenore E. A. 1979. *The Battered Woman.* New York: Harper and Row.

Walker Lenore E. A. 1991. "Post Traumatic Stress Disorder in Battered Women: Diagnosis and Treatment of Battered Women's Syndrome." *Psychotherapy* 28: 21-9.

Walker Lenore E. A. 1993. "The Battered Woman Syndrome Is A Psychological Consequence of Abuse." Pp. 133-53 in *Current Controversies on Family Violence*, edited by Richard J. Gelles and Donileen R. Loseke. Newbury Park, California: Sage.

Walker Lenore E. A. 1994. *Abused Women and Survivor Therapy: A Practical Guide for the Psychotherapist.* Washington D.C.: American Psychological Association.

Walker Lenore E. A. 1999. "Battered Woman Syndrome and Self

Defense." *Notre Dame Journal of Law and Ethics and Public Policy* 6:321-34.

Waxman, L. and S. Hinderliter. 1996. *A Status Report on Hun* ger and Homelessness in America's Cities. Washington D.C.: U.S. Conference of Mayors.

Weldon Michele. 1999. *I Closed My Eyes: Revelations of a Battered Woman*. Garden City: Hazelden.

Wethington Elaine and Ronald C. Kessler. 1986. "Perceived Support, Received Support, and Adjustment to Stressful Life Events." *Journal of Health and Social Behavior* 27 (3):78-89.

Wilson Charles. 1998. "Are Battered Women Responsible for Protection of their Children in Domestic Violence Cases?" *Journal of Interpersonal Violence* 13 (2):289-93.

Wilson John P. 1984. "A Comparative Analysis of Post Traumatic Stress Syndrome." *Journal of Sociology and Social Welfare* 11 (4):793-825.

Winner Karen. 1996. *Divorced From Justice: The Abuse of Women and Children by Divorce Lawyers and Judges*. New York: Harper Collins

Yilo Kersti A. 1993. "Through A Feminist Lens: Gender, Power and Violence." Pp. 47-62 in *Current Controversies on Family Violence,* edited by Richard J. Gelles and Donileen R. Loseke. Newbury Park: Sage.

Zorza Joan. 1991. "Woman Battering: A Major Cause of Homelessness." *Clearinghouse Review.* 25:421

Zorza Joan. 1995. *Guide to Interstate Custody: A Manual for Domestic Violence Advocates*. New York: National Battered Women's Law Project

How Battered Women Stay Out

APPENDIX A

FINDING LONG TERM SURVIVORS

What is a "Long Term Survivor"?

My first step, for the purposes of this study, was to define, what a "long term survivor" was. It was also necessary to formulate very specific definitions for the terms "exit", "mate", and "abuse". I reviewed prior literature in depth, and also used feedback from other survivors along with own intuitive processes and experience. After careful forethought, I would define "long term survivor" as: "*a woman who has exited a relationship, involving emotional and physical abuse from a spouse or domestic partner, and has not returned to cohabitation with this person, for a period of at least three years*".

"Exit" was initially defined as: *leaving the abusive household or as forcing the abuser to leave*. As the interviews progressed however, it became apparent to me that some survivors had experienced multiple relationships which included both physical and emotional abuse. Because of this, I needed to establish a common survivor "exit" point. I designated this point as: *the first time the survivor left an abusive "mate"*.

A "mate", for the purposes of my interviews, would be: *the first abusive husband or domestic partner with whom the survivor had lived with, independently, after leaving their home*.

The three year minimum time gone from the abuser was chosen for this study because most of the prior research on battered women had included only the brief period after women left abusers or shelters. In rare cases, such as those highlighted in a previous Chapter (Hoff 1990; Goetting 1999) survivors were interviewed after they had been gone for more than a year. I also knew that a very high rate of attempted reconciliations exist in relationships involving domestic violence, and as many as five successive returns to the abuser, particularly within the first two years after women left (Goetting 1999). I decided that establishing a *minimum "time gone", after the "exit," of three years* would indicate that the abuse survivor had terminated the relationship, permanently, or at least, it would imply a sincere effort to avoid going back to the abuser. Studies on the process of uncoupling, and on grief, have also shown that permanently ending a relationship, subjectively, can take 5-8 years (Jacobsen 1986). Although partners may have legally ended a marriage, and may, even, live miles away from one another, emotions such as anger and resentment may persist and take a long time to resolve (Goetting 1999).

Finally, "physical abuse" was loosely defined as: *the intentional, willful, infliction of physical injury, on another, by hitting, beating, shoving and/or pushing.* "Emotional abuse" was defined as: *the infliction of emotional hurt by using degrading remarks, insults, dominating behavior, threats, silence and/or isolation*

Selecting Survivors

The selection of the women I would interview was scientifically " purposeful and deliberate", based on the parameters I had delineated in my working definitions of the terms "long term survivor", "exit" and "abuse". I was also interested in diversity of age, time gone from the abuser, income level, race, and ethnicity. I used, what is known as, a purposive sampling method, which included distributing flyers, posting bulletins, and announcements. I also mentioned my search for survivors of domestic abuse during casual conversations with business and social contacts. Letters and phone calls were made to domestic violence agencies in several attempts to recruit survivors. Announcements at two college campuses led to four respondents so in an attempt to further diversify the survivors in educational level and experience, the remainder of interviews came from other sources and locations. My final group of long term survivors would consist of sixteen women from Ventura and Los Angeles Counties in California. Twelve women were drawn from the general community. One of the twelve survivors from the community was employed at a domestic violence agency at the time of her interview. Another woman was staying in a homeless shelter. Other women were referred to me through friends, as well as by informal and business contacts. As mentioned earlier, four women were recruited from college populations. Most of the women, in both the community and student populations, were employed, either full or part-time. Eight women were Anglo-American, four women were Latina, and four women were African American.

During over a year of continuing interview sessions, I would explore in great depth with these strong, courageous women, the various challenges, obstacles, problems and successes they had experienced over time. I found that these survivors had been gone, from what they stated to be their first abusive mates, from 3 to 40 years with the median time being 13 years (mean: 14.8 years). Only five women had been gone for less than ten years. Six survivors were physically or psychologically disabled from gainful employment. Those interview respondents, the long term survivors, themselves, were introduced to you, and described further in Chapter 3. In the Chapters that followed, readers were able to learn more about the many insights they gained, along the way, as well as the various skills they developed – and even more importantly, to benefit from the wisdom we all can gain as a result of hearing from them

I began to conduct a long series of in-depth, semi-structured interviews with all of the long term survivors.[2] My initial interview with each woman lasted a total of from two to five hours. Follow-up sessions were scheduled, and completed, when necessary. Repeat visits were necessary in only two cases. I utilized a loosely designed schedule of open ended questions. These questions were designed to address both the problems and the successes women had experienced, beginning with the day they first left an abusive mate. (see Appendix C for my interview schedule) Survivors were questioned further about what long-term problems, if any, they had experienced after their departures (or "post exit"). Potential-

---

[2] The goal of my study was to point to patterns and meanings among survivors, rather than to generalize to a larger population, so I used an inductive, in-depth approach. My interviews were conducted with a small group of survivors in order to validate and learn from the survivors' experience, not to validate large statistics (Reinharz 1992). Please see Appendix A for more details.

ly, problematic issues, such as housing, protection, safety, child support, child custody, medical condition, repeat victimization, and ongoing family and social interactions were addressed in depth. Survivors were also questioned about the perceived availability and effectiveness of informal and formal support systems, such as friends, relatives, clergy, shelter or community services, police, legal advocates, government agencies, and the like.

Keeping with the semi-structured interview approach, my interview sessions proceeded as, what could be called, "guided conversations", where women's particular and sometimes, unexpected responses often influenced and directed the specific content of the interview (Berg 1998). I also used probing questions, based on each survivor's most important concerns, during the time that had passed since they left their abusers (Schwartz and Jacobs 1979). Using the basics of feminist and grounded theory analysis, I asked each survivor to answer questions that were designed beforehand, or even, sometimes, spontaneously created, in order to address their own specific problems, concerns, and needs, after leaving abusers. Women were, also, encouraged to elaborate on the particular aspects of their own unique experience that had impacted *them* the most were encouraged to explore the *meaning,* significance and potential effect of social support from others (or lack thereof) in their lives.

At the end of the interview, each woman was asked for her own subjective definition of what it meant to be a "Survivor" of domestic violence and abuse. Women were also encouraged to describe what a "Survivor" was, *in contrast* to what a "Victim" was. Did they think there was any actual, significant difference between the two terms or labels? Their responses would emerge as varied, thought provoking and interesting. Asking the above questions, at the end of each interview session, allowed survivors to frame their responses, through a fresh recall of the feelings, experiences, and survival strategies they had related to me earlier. By this time, the survivors were also more comfortable with talking to me, and, in many cases, more spontaneous in their replies. I anticipated that, had these same questions been asked in the earlier stages of the interview, I would have a more limited guarded, objective, academic, or a less subjectively informed response from respondents.

Some might argue that sharing my own personal experiences with survivors during our sessions, could risk, or even destroy my ability to be objective. In direct contradiction, other experts would insist that by recognizing, and even increasing subjectivity, a researcher's objectivity can actually be *increased.* These experts believe that, *by not hiding* the researcher's own personal experience, an ideal circumstance for enhanced discovery can be created, uncovering findings that might, otherwise, be overlooked (Harding, 1987).

Methods and Analysis

Coding and analysis of my interview data were conducted using, what sociologists call a "grounded theory" approach (see next section: Glaser and Strauss 1967; Strauss and Corbin 1990). Themes which emerged from the survivors' own experience, as they described it, were later identified, coded, and analyzed, after my repeated reviews of the interview text. I purposely delayed data analysis until after the first ten interviews were collected. I made the decision to delay analysis until this point in order to allow myself to first absorb what I anticipated (correctly), to be a vast diversity among women's' experiences. As the interviews and my analysis progressed, recurrent themes began to emerge from their stories, which allowed for later comparisons. As broader patterns emerged from the data and became repetitive, I was then able to look at the corresponding, contrasting, and conflicting phenomena in the long term survivors' experience. Reading pertinent literature before, during, and after my interviews both enhanced and validated recurrent emergent themes, as well as adding to theoretical sensitivity (Strauss and Corbin 1990).

Limitations of This Study

This study of long term survivors is not large enough to be scientifically generalized to larger populations. That was not my intention. Since my primary concern was exploring both the objective and subjective realities that long term survivors experience, I combined "grounded theory" approach" with feminist methodolo-

191

gy. This research approach would encapsulate for me the *meanings* women applied to being a survivor. It would allow me to explore the feelings they experienced along the way, and the unique strategies that they employed as survivors after they left their abusers. In grounded theory, analysis evolves through the experience of those we study. It is inspired by the Chicago School tradition of entering the field, conducting intensive in-depth interviews, and capturing the subject's social reality through up-close observation (Glaser and Strauss 1967; Strauss and Corbin 1990). This form of exploration of the unique and shared experiences of domestic violence survivors would enable me to develop what researchers and ethnographers call *sensitizing concepts* (Blumer 1969). These concepts can ultimately develop into themes that represent the meanings of things in a person' or persons' lives and the actions they tended to take.

Since the goal of conducting my interviews with survivors was to point out patterns and meanings rather than to generalize to a larger population, I believe it was very appropriate, as well as successful, due to its inductive, in-depth approach. My study of survivors was primarily designed to validate the survivors' experience, not to validate statistics (Reinharz 1992). In fact, the major limitation to my research, as presented it at this writing, may be the fact that these women's stories were not allowed to stand "as is," unhampered by analysis, as pure, raw biographies of women who have survived abuse. Their stories contain both rich narratives and valuable information. As members of a historically oppressed and overlooked group, these long term survivors had been silent for many years, and now, they have finally spoken.

Excluded Groups

Since those survivors who allowed themselves to be interviewed did so voluntarily, this study also excludes the experience of the many women who were *not* approached for an interview, as well as those who *would have not* volunteered. Other important subgroups of women, who have survived abuse, have also been excluded from this sample because of time, demographics, and funding constraints. For instance, we do not hear in this study from women in prison who are also "survivors", in some cases, perhaps only, because they have killed their abusive mates. Other survivors of domestic abuse are also currently incarcerated due to crimes they have committed, as a reaction to, or as a result of the relationship with their abusers. We also do not hear, in this book, from other sub-groups of women who represent the broad spectrum of those victims who have become survivors of abuse, such as the invisible abused homeless, those abused women who are now housed in mental institutions and on the other end of the social spectrum, those women who are members of historically economically advantaged groups. (for a further discussion of overlooked populations, please see Appendix B: Suggestions for Further Research).

Ethical Concerns

The women I interviewed were assured of total confidentiality. This is especially important when interviewing victims of abuse due to the potential of perceived or real threat to their well being. Like me, three of the women I interviewed were still in hiding from their abusers. All of the survivors were assured that their own names would be replaced with pseudonyms and that geographic location, past or present, job titles of themselves, names of their children or their abusers and any other relevant information would be also altered.

When interviewing women who have undergone mental and physical abuse, authors, or social researchers must also remain aware of the potential of the survivor reliving, or re- experiencing, unpleasant memories of the past or trauma. Respondents were reminded in writing and verbally, that they could decline to answer any question or questions that I asked. They were also reminded that they could pause, stop, or end the interview at any time. I used considerable care in ascertaining that women were comfortable throughout the interview. I also allowed each woman to be the ultimate determinant of how much detail she wanted to add about emotionally charged circumstances in her life. Many of the women I interviewed would express an array of powerful emotions such as anger, frustration, and exhilaration and in some cases, considerable grief. Anticipating this possibility, at the end of each interview, I also provided survivors with a list of resources for low cost or sliding fee counseling, should they need them.

It was very interesting to me to discover that every single one of the survivors I interviewed did choose to explain to me, in various degrees, the abuse they had suffered at the hand of their mates. Although women were not encouraged or required to describe these "events" again, since my focus was on their experience after they left, they did *choose* to talk about the acts of abuse they had experienced. Sometimes they spoke at length about them. Whether to validate their victimization, for cathartic relief, or just to share "war stories", these survivor "warrior women" described the abuse they had suffered, often in depth. Because some survivors had also been victims of child abuse, raw accounts of these situations were also sometimes related to me. The occurrences of abuse in some women's life histories seemed to nearly blend with one another. In only one case, was it necessary to end the interview prematurely and to proceed, weeks later, when the survivor called me on the phone and invited me to come and talk with her again.

Many women expressed very positive feelings about finally having an opportunity to explain both the problems and the successes that they had experienced since they left their abusers. I am pleased to say that I was able to maintain contact with all but one of the women that I interviewed. Some of the other survivors have also written or called me. All of the survivors who I spoke with were willing, at the time, to be available for further communication or interview sessions either in-person, or by written or telephone contact in the future. Two of the survivors, "Dorothy" and "Yvonne", have since passed away. These brave women are memorialized after Chapter 12 of this book. I think of them very often, so grateful that their voices can still be heard and their wisdom forever shared on these pages.

APPENDIX B

SUGGESTIONS FOR FUTURE RESEARCH

It is my opinion that what survivors described to me as the "aspired to" states of Normalcy, Mastery, and Recovery are particularly interesting avenues for further research in this area. As the findings in this book indicate, these "ways of being" appeared to define for the survivors I spoke with, their long-term experiences, their goal-seeking behavior, and even their conceptualization of survival "per se". As a result, gaining normalcy, mastery, and recovery directed the actions *and* problem solving efforts of each survivor to one degree or another as time "away" progressed. Understanding better how these areas are related to a domestic violence survivor's particular needs would better illuminate how she ultimately seeks and delineates support at various junctures in her life. Also, of significant interest was the predominant tendency for survivors to reject or avoid "being judged" by potential support providers. Further analysis of how a social support provider's ability to empathize, to avoid judgment, or in sociological terms to "role-take" (Meloy 1993) affects interaction between survivors and members of both informal and formal support systems might provide valuable insights.

The ability to speak with and to later survey a much larger sample of long term survivors would also be very valuable. The sample could be expanded to include women who have the potential of being overlooked in typical research settings (see Appendix A: Excluded Groups). Conducting interviews with battered women who did not kill their abusers, but who are now incarcerated in jails, for various other offenses, would provide a unique view of the role that problem solving ability, self-evaluation, and social support played in their own particular experiences. Other long term survivors who may be overlooked could also be located among chronically homeless populations or in both in-patient, and out-patient, mental health and addiction treatment programs. It would be very valuable to determine the particular survival strategies that these women employed, after they left their abusers, along with the role of informal and formal support systems and the reflected appraisal of others in their particular experience (see Richie 1996). In contrast, talking to long term survivors who are *financially advantaged* would also provide data about how this subgroup of survivors, who are typically perceived to have superior

195

material and social resources, obtained and actually experienced social support, over the long term.

Another valuable area for future research would be studies designed to explore the experience of the children of long term survivors of domestic abuse. Children are often profoundly affected by the experience, as well as the aftermath, of violence in the home. Witnessing their mothers being beaten and verbally abused, or being abused, themselves, as children, can create emotional scars that are very difficult to overcome. After their mothers leave, as this study has shown, the problems of children can be compounded by their mother's poverty, by her repeat victimization, by her trauma or fears, or by their inability to know their fathers, which can create feelings of guilt, confusion, and anger. Understanding the particular difficulties these children face as survivors, in the attempt to redefine their own lives, could uncover very valuable data for those who wish to address potential generational patterns of abuse.

APPENDIX C

SAMPLE INTERVIEW SCHEDULE

I would like to know what life has been like for you since you left your abuser.

1. How long ago did you leave him?

2. When you actually decided to leave, what was your first concern? What did you need?

3. What did you decide to do about the concerns or needs?

4. Did you turn to anyone for help with these concerns and needs?

5. How effective was the assistance given? Why or why not?

6. If the assistance was ineffective, what other solutions did you use to try and solve the problem?

7. What other needs/problems, connected to your former abuse, did you have after you left your abuser?

I continued to repeat Questions 3, 4, 5, 6, 7 in a generally chronological order, allowing respondent to talk freely about the issues and/or areas of concern that have most significantly impacted her life. Continue probing until all of the potential issues below have been exhausted:

> Protection, Safety, Physical Injury
> Legal Issues, Child Custody, Visitation
> Housing problems, Homelessness
> Financial Problems, Poverty
> Family and Social Interaction
> Emotional, Psychological Problems
> Child Rearing, Behavioral Problems
> Communication Problems
> Subsequent Mental or Physical Abuse

8. How do you think your life has been affected by your prior abuse? In what particular ways?

9. What is the difference is between a survivor and a victim - or do you think there is a difference?

10. What, if anything, that is connected with your prior abuse, do you still need assistance for now?

11. Have you attempted to obtain any assistance for this/these problems? What particular obstacles or challenges have you faced in your attempts to gain assistance?

12. What successes are you most proud of since you left your abuser.

14. Who/what has been most helpful to you over the long term in surviving abuse? (for instance:, friends, family, church, women's groups, shelter, new friends, new partner, classes, books, legal assistance, courts, police, government agencies etc.)

15. Do you have any suggestions for those who want to do more to really help domestic violence survivors and their children?

ABOUT THE AUTHOR

Mary Walker Owens, also a survivor of domestic violence, has been writing, publishing, and facilitating the work of other writers and artists, for over forty years. She obtained her Master's Degrees in Family Sociology from California State University Northridge. She also has taught Sociology of the Family, Sociology of Mental Health and Deviance, as well as Criminology at both CSU Northridge and Channel Islands Universities. She is also an accomplished fine artist and spent several years as an Art Facilitator/Therapist. Ms Owens has authored several articles on social issues such as domestic violence and mental health issues. Her acclaimed qualitative case study of an aging Midwest gay HIV survivor earned her the prestigious Sage Society Award and a generous cash endowment toward future research. Mary has also been published in newspapers, edited several newsletters, authored sales manuals and promotional literature, and written several works of prose, poetry and drama.

Currently residing in Las Vegas Nevada, Ms. Owens recently co-edited the esteemed "In Full Bloom" Creative Journal for the Osher Institute at the University of Nevada at Las Vegas. She has also recently become owner and Managing Editor for her own company, GREAT SKY PUBLISHING. She is convinced that she is now engaged in her most important mission in life: that of helping other writers self-publish high quality books. She is now providing a real opportunity for those voices that might otherwise be unnoticed, ignored, or unpublished, to be heard, read, recognized, and celebrated. Ms. Owens can be contacted by email at greatskypub@aol.com or through her website address which is: www.greatskypub.com

WRITE YOUR BOOK

TELL YOUR STORY

CREATE A LEGACY

✺

GREAT SKY PUBLISHING

www.greatskypub.com

greatskypub@aol.com

SIA information can be obtained at www.ICGtesting.com
Printed in the USA
LVOW10s1723040914

402458LV00023B/1327/P

9 781497 502994